THE HILLS

CITY OF ANGELS

THE HILLS

CITY OF ANGELS

ANDREW PERRY

NEW YORK   LONDON   TORONTO   SYDNEY

POCKET BOOKS, a division of Simon & Schuster, Inc.
1230 Avenue of the Americas, New York, NY 10020

ISBN- 13: 978-1-4165-3757-1
ISBN-10:   1-4165-3757-0

First MTV Books/Pocket Books trade paperback edition November 2006

10   9   8   7   6   5   4   3   2   1

POCKET and colophon are registered trademarks of
Simon & Schuster, Inc.

Manufactured in the United States of America

For information regarding special discounts for bulk purchases,
please contact Simon & Schuster Special Sales at 1-800-456-6798
or business@simonandschuster.com

The Girls from the Hills

Lauren

Hometown: Laguna Beach, Orange County

Major: Product Development at FIDM

Dream job: Opening up her own boutique, designing and selling her creations—wants to be her own boss (like her dad)

Guilty of: Messiness

Feels naked without: Eyeliner

Being on her own: Loves the independence

Fears: Nothing intimidates her

Heidi

Hometown: Crested Butte, Colorado, but she's not a small-town person

Dream job: Working in the entertainment industry
Best feature: Outgoing
Greatest fear: Missing out in life
Guilty of: Being the most flirtatious person you'll ever meet
If she could change one thing: Would be more open and accepting
Motto: "Live every day as if it were your last, because it just might be."

Whitney

Hometown: Brentwood, Los Angeles—went to the same high school as Kate Hudson and Jack Black
Major: Gender Studies
Dream job: Opening up her own boutique
Self-proclaimed: Romantic
Being on her own: Lives with four other girls, misses her mom's cooking
Admires: Her sisters
Motto: "Don't worry, be happy."

Audrina

Hometown: Yorba Linda, Orange County

Dream job: Modeling and acting

Hates: Being alone—the biggest adjustment in moving to L.A. was living by herself

Best feature: Gets the most compliments on her eyes

Bet you didn't know: Has a tattoo on the back of her neck, a heart that turns into an apple with a snake wrapped around it

Motto: "Go big or go home."

THE HILLS

CITY OF ANGELS

Just Like a Girl
from Back Home

Lauren and Heidi

It seemed like it had rained every day since Lauren had moved to San Francisco from Laguna Beach, having come to the city to study fashion and design at the Academy of Art University. The city and the college weren't exactly what she had expected or hoped.

Lauren had chosen the school for its design program and because it was in San Francisco, far enough away from Laguna, but not *too* far. After all, she was a California girl at heart.

Heidi was a Colorado girl who wanted to live in a big city; she especially loved the idea of being able to walk everywhere. She visited New York City colleges, but found the city overwhelming and uninviting. San Francisco, on the other hand, felt smaller, hip, and more manageable.

The first day of college can be nerve-wracking—being a stranger on a strange campus, where everyone seems to know where they're going except you. First-day jitters were made even worse by other anxieties. Had Lauren done the right thing in moving to San Francisco? Did Heidi really want to go to fashion school?

Each girl walked into class that morning unsure if she had made the right choice. It didn't help that every other girl in the

classroom looked like a punk or a goth or some combination of the two. Heidi looked around the room and saw no one she even wanted to talk to—which was a rare thing for Heidi. But then she saw Lauren. Her long, wavy blond hair stood out in a room of teased-out punky dark hair, and her outfit was cute and fashionable. Heidi thought, *She looks like someone I'd know back home.*

Lauren, too, was feeling like she was trapped in a freak show. All the other girls seemed to be wearing sculpted frowns. Is this what college was going to be like? Rain and a bunch of angry punk girls? Then Lauren noticed a cute short blond girl walking over to her. She seemed friendly and approachable, someone you could have a coffee with and share your secrets. Just like someone Lauren might have known back home.

"Hi, want to be my friend?" Heidi introduced herself to Lauren in her typically blunt way.

"Uh, sure," Lauren said.

Any other time, Lauren might have interpreted Heidi's question as a completely uncool move, something that only someone desperate would do. But as she scanned the room of goth girls again, Lauren felt a little desperate herself. At that moment, Heidi's blunt question was the best offer she'd had all day.

The professor walked into the classroom and asked everyone to take his/her seats.

"My name's Heidi," Heidi whispered quickly.

"I'm Lauren."

After class, the two girls picked up where they had left off.

As it turned out, Heidi was hardly desperate. She was funny and down-to-earth and hated the weather in San Francisco as much as Lauren did. Lauren felt like she had finally met someone she could relate to, and Heidi felt the same. They decided to share a cab back to their apartments, which were just a couple of blocks apart. Needless to say, it was the beginning of a beautiful friendship. After their first semester, the two friends had enough of AAU and San Francisco, and decided to take their chances in Los Angeles.

Lauren's Favorite Things About San Francisco

1. Caffé Grecco

2. The view from Coit Tower

3. De Young Museum and Golden Gate Park

4. Greens Restaurant

5. Mario's Bohemian Cigar Store and Cafe

Good-bye, New York

Jordan and Brian

Jordan and Brian loved living in the New York City area. They were getting work in New York—not a ton of work, but enough to survive. They spent their days auditioning for modeling and acting jobs and at night it was all about hitting the right clubs, searching for the perfect party, and meeting the hottest girls.

But commuting was a drag. Brian had an apartment in Queens, where he'd grown up, and Jordan was shuffling back and forth each day to his place in New Jersey. They were eager to live in the middle of the action: Manhattan. After their auditions were over one day, they looked at apartments, hoping to find something they could afford that was at least livable—not easy when you were making just enough to get by. Neither of them spent all that much time at his apartment, and they imagined their new place would be just for sleeping.

They looked at a few places in the hippest neighborhoods, like the Lower East Side and Nolita, but everything was way too expensive for them. They didn't want to give up on the idea of being roommates, but the housing options in Manhattan weren't looking too good.

On the train back home to New Jersey that night, Jordan got a call from his friend James, who lived in Los Angeles. Jordan was feeling depressed and discouraged, and James made living in L.A. sound like paradise. There were so many more work opportunities for actors in Hollywood than in New York, James explained. He also told Jordan how the music scene was bigger and easier to break into. He didn't want to ever leave L.A.

After Jordan got off the phone with James, a plan sparked in his mind. What if, instead of finding a place in Manhattan, Jordan and Brian moved to Los Angeles? Jordan had wanted to make it in the music business since he was a little kid. Maybe L.A. was the way to follow his musical dreams. He called up Brian, and they talked about it excitedly. It turned out that Brian, too, had been thinking about a move to California, but hadn't mentioned it to Jordan.

The very next day they figured out how to make the move. They decided Brian would ship his car, and then they would drive to California in Jordan's car. But first, there were a few loose ends to wrap up in New York. They were both represented by the same talent agency, so they each made a call to their agents to tell them about the plan. The agents were all for it and said they'd talk to their colleagues at the Los Angeles office so that Jordan and Brian could have representation when they arrived. That was a huge coup. It meant that when they got to Hollywood, they wouldn't have to spend any time looking for new agents.

James said they could crash at his apartment in L.A. until Jordan and Brian found a place to live on their own. With everything falling into place, Jordan was now convinced that the move was meant to happen.

They threw a good-bye party at Brian's apartment, and all their New York friends were there. When the party was at its height, someone raised a glass and yelled, "We're gonna miss you guys. Good luck out there." Everyone cheered. Brian and Jordan knew they were going to miss their friends and the scene in New York, but it was time to take this shot at living their dreams. The following day Jordan and Brian packed up Jordan's car and took off for California.

One thing Jordan and Brian agreed on was to make their trip

across the country a leisurely one. They weren't on anyone's timetable but their own. If they wanted to visit friends or relatives on the way or play miniature golf next to a big concrete purple hippopotamus, they would.

Brian wanted to check out kooky roadside attractions, while Jordan was on a quest to find the perfect hamburger. Each was happy to go along for the ride on the other guy's journey, especially since they might never have such an opportunity again. If that meant an hour out of the way for the Museum of Pez (Brian) or a detour to see Colonel Sanders's grave site (Jordan), they did it.

Besides having fun, the guys were psyched about their careers. Jordan really wanted to put all his energy into his music and Brian wanted to take his acting to the next level, movies. It felt like the world was theirs for the taking.

After a couple of weeks of tourist traps, greasy fast food, and roadside oddities, they crossed the border into California. Both guys let out a whoop of excitement. They had made it! They drove on to Los Angeles in silence, wondering what awaited them. This was their chance to make their dreams come true.

Jordan and Brian seeing the sights in Las Vegas.

Jordan and Brian's Favorite Cross-Country Attractions

1. Grand Canyon
2. Mount Rushmore
3. Sonny Bono's grave
4. Four Corners
5. Caesar's Palace in Las Vegas

Second Chance at a First Impression

Heidi and Jordan

Before they moved to Los Angeles, Lauren and Heidi spent some time there to figure out where they wanted to live and go to school. Lauren devoted most of her time to practical matters, while Heidi, naturally, focused on her top priority: the party scene.

There's always a party in Hollywood, if you know where to look. Everyone knows about nightclubs and after-hours clubs, of course, but the best parties are house parties, where you need to know who's throwing the party—or at least know someone who knows the person throwing it.

Heidi and Lauren had been going out a lot on this trip. Heidi loved the nightlife, but Lauren had to admit she was getting weary of it all as she felt the stress of everything she had to get done. Didn't Heidi ever get stressed? It didn't seem so.

It had been a blistering hot day, and as they were getting ready for their night out, Lauren had her doubts about how enjoyable it was going to be.

"Are you sure you know where the party is this time?" she asked Heidi.

"I'm sure," Heidi said, applying her makeup.

"The last time you said that, we ended up in the Valley," Lauren pointed out.

"At least we got In-N-Out Burger, though," Heidi said wistfully.

"In-N-Out is everywhere, Heidi," Lauren said. "We don't need to go all the way to the Valley."

"I know where we're going tonight," Heidi insisted.

The girls finished getting ready and then left in Lauren's car. Heidi had the address written on a piece of paper, and, unlike two nights ago, this evening she remembered to bring it along in the car with her.

They drove into the Hills and luckily they found the party quite easily. The entire neighborhood was jammed with cars, and Lauren could only find a place to park a good half-mile from the house.

They walked into the crowded party, and Heidi instantly saw ten people she hadn't seen in *forever*, which for Heidi meant about a week. This always happened when they went to parties. Heidi knew everyone there. If she didn't know them, by the end of the night they would all be her new best friends.

Lauren was a little jealous of the ease Heidi had with social interactions, but tonight the feeling evaporated when Lauren spotted a girl she knew from Laguna Beach. She went over to say hi, knowing Heidi would have no trouble navigating the party on her own.

Sure enough, within moments Heidi was talking with her friend Christine. Christine was already jetting off to another party, but really wanted Heidi to meet another friend of hers.

"He's the cutest guy," Christine said. "I think you guys would totally, I mean *totally*, hit it off."

"Sure, point him out," Heidi said playfully.

Christine scanned the main room, but didn't see him. Since she was about to leave, she told Heidi what the guy in question looked like so that Heidi could keep an eye out for him. According to Christine, his hair was dark blond, he was wearing a blue shirt, and his name was Jordan. And with that she hugged Heidi and made her exit.

Heidi looked around the room for Lauren, but didn't see her. Lauren usually enjoyed herself at parties, but Heidi still liked to check in with her now and then throughout the evening to make sure she was having a good time; that's what friends are for.

Heidi wandered into the kitchen, which was packed, as it always seems to be at parties. Heidi didn't see Lauren and was about to leave to check the next room when someone caught her eye. A guy with dark blond hair and a blue shirt was standing by the back door, making out with a girl. Really going at it, with groping and everything. Heidi raised her eyebrows. *Is that the guy Christine wanted me to meet?* There was only one way to find out. In the middle of the crowded room, Heidi yelled out, "Jordan!" And sure enough, the guy stopped making out for a second and looked up. But when he didn't see anyone he knew in the room, he went back to chewing the girl's lips.

Heidi immediately decided two things: One, the guy was a loser, and two, Christine needed a phone call. Heidi punched Christine's numbers into her cell phone. There was no answer, so Heidi left a message thanking Christine for the guy suggestion, but letting her know she wasn't into him after all. When Heidi finally found Lauren, the two girls decided the party was lame and made a hasty retreat.

Two nights later Heidi was out again, and she had completely forgotten about the Jordan incident. But while she was at Spider, dancing with friends, she spotted Jordan sitting on a stool by the bar. At first she wasn't even sure if it was the same guy. He had on a different shirt, and he didn't have a girl attached to his lips. He was just sitting there, staring at Heidi.

Heidi thought she might have been mistaken about his interest in her, but when she looked back a few seconds later, he was still staring. Finally he got off the stool and started walking toward her and her friends on the dance floor. When he reached her, he said, "Hi, I'm Jordan."

"I know," Heidi said, as she kept dancing, determined not to lose her cool.

"I'm a friend of Christine's."

Heidi nodded, wondering how he knew who she was. Never shy to ask questions, she said, "How'd you know what I looked like?"

"Christine showed me a picture of you on her cell phone a few nights ago. And then when someone yelled out my name at the party the other night, I figured it was you."

Heidi's face flushed. So much for playing it cool.

"Do you think maybe we could start over and meet like normal people?" he asked.

"Where's your make-out buddy?" Heidi asked.

"That was really nothing. Can I buy you a drink?"

Heidi stopped dancing. She didn't want a drink, but she liked the way Jordan was handling himself.

"I need a break," she said.

She walked off the dance floor. Jordan didn't follow her until she motioned with her finger for him to do so. They sat down

together in one of the padded booths lining the walls of the club.

As they began talking, Heidi discovered, to her surprise, that Jordan was very courteous and not the lame jerk she had originally thought him to be. Jordan told her that he had been in Los Angeles only a couple of weeks and was still getting a feel for the place. He admitted to being homesick sometimes, but said that he spoke to his parents a lot, and found comfort in his religion.

Heidi was taken aback. Family and religion? Jordan definitely wasn't like most of the guys she had met, who were just trying to get her into bed as fast as they could. Heidi truly sensed something different in him. They ended up talking the entire evening, absorbed in conversation until it was time to go.

As they were saying good night in front of the club, Jordan asked for Heidi's number. She gave it to him, along with a little kiss on the cheek. Bursting with excitement, Heidi skipped all the way to her car.

Heidi's Advice for Finding a Guy in Los Angeles

1. There are a lot of fake people in Los Angeles, but there are also a lot of really genuine people. Try the genuine people first.

2. If that doesn't work, move on to the fake people.

3. The best relationship advice I ever got was: Don't be afraid to go after what you want.

4. On a first date, always have a rescue call planned. It's the perfect escape from a bad date.

Reunited and It Feels So Good

Whitney and David

Whitney and her boyfriend, David, met when they were in middle school in Brentwood. It was the beginning of seventh grade, and Whitney, an Angeleno native, spotted David, the new kid in class, right away. She thought he was cute and made a point to know him better. After a few weeks, she realized she had an out-and-out crush on him. She didn't do anything about it, though, which was unusual for her. Most of the time, if

Whitney liked somebody at school, she would promptly tell her friends and her parents, but for some reason Whitney kept the crush she had on David a secret. Maybe her feelings for David were just too special to share.

Whitney's crush on David outlasted seventh grade, although nothing ever came of it. Whitney would see David in the halls and think, *That's a cute boy.* But schoolwork and after-school activities took up most of Whitney's time, and eventually she gave up on her crush.

After high school, Whitney left L.A. to attend the University of Colorado, Boulder, where she planned to major in gender studies. Meanwhile, David was off to the University of California—Berkeley, to study communications.

But after a year in Colorado, Whitney decided Boulder was way too cold for her and she didn't like being so far away from home, so she transferred to the University of Southern California in Los Angeles.

At a party one night at USC, Whitney learned from a high school friend that David had transferred from Berkeley and that he was also attending USC. Recalling her middle school crush, she wondered if she'd bump into him on campus. A few days later, Whitney's friend had a birthday party and told her that David was also invited.

Whitney was nervous about seeing David after so much time, but she didn't tell anyone about her nerves. She decided to just see how things went, and tried not to worry about it.

Whitney saw David the minute she entered the party. To her surprise, he rushed over to greet her, giving her a warm hug. They both admitted they had been out of touch way too long and launched into a long conversation about the past, the present, and everything in between. Before they knew it, they were the last ones at the party. They had completely lost track of everything going on around them. Whitney apologized to her friend the next day, worried that she might have seemed rude. The friend didn't care; she just wanted to know what happened with David. Whitney admitted that she and David had exchanged numbers.

It looked like Whitney's schoolgirl crush from years ago was about to blossom into a relationship. David called Whitney the next day, and soon they were seeing a lot of each other. Who knew your seventh-grade crush could turn into your college boyfriend?

Checking the Box

Heidi and Jordan

After they officially met at Spider, Jordan called Heidi the next day and politely asked if he could see her again. She agreed, eager to pick up where they'd left off.

That night they went to Joseph's in Hollywood. Lauren came along to meet Heidi's new guy. Jordan seemed a bit quiet to Lauren, but nice.

The evening went extremely well. Heidi knew a lot of people at the club, and she also met a few of Jordan's friends, including his roommate, Brian. At the end of the night, Jordan didn't want to say good-bye, and neither did Heidi. She couldn't believe she was having such a great time with this guy she'd originally thought was a jerk.

Jordan walked Heidi out to her car. They leaned against the car and kept talking, unwilling to let the night end. Then, because she couldn't wait any longer, Heidi kissed him. It was a good kiss—Jordan knew what he was doing, unlike some of the lame-o's Heidi had kissed in the past. When their lips parted, Heidi was glad that their first real kiss was over with. Sometimes a guy could take forever to kiss you, and Heidi hated waiting around for that, especially if it was guy she really liked—and she really liked Jordan.

Finally Jordan said good night and Heidi got into her car. She immediately called Lauren and told her she was waiting for her in the parking lot. Lauren said good-bye to the people she had been talking to inside the club and went outside. As soon as she was in the car, Heidi said, "I like him. I really like him."

Lauren was pleased for Heidi; she deserved a good guy like Jordan. All the way home, Heidi couldn't stop talking about him and Lauren thought that was adorable.

Heidi and Jordan became inseparable, but soon Jordan had to go back home to North Carolina for his brother's wedding, and Heidi and Lauren had to settle things in San Francisco so they could move to L.A. Heidi and Jordan hadn't formalized their relationship in any way, although they spent every waking hour together, and most sleeping hours, too. (At one point Brian joked that he hadn't seen Jordan in three days and was going to send out a search and rescue team.)

Jordan didn't want to go back home without knowing what to call his relationship with Heidi. He wanted to call her his girlfriend, but he also didn't want to turn it into some huge thing. The truth was, he *already* thought of Heidi as his girlfriend; he just didn't know if she thought of him as her boyfriend. Jordan decided to send Heidi flowers the day he left for the wedding. He knew she loved lilies, so he sent her a giant bouquet of them along with a note that said: *Will you be my girlfriend? Check Yes or No*, beneath which he had drawn two little boxes.

Brian was driving Jordan to the airport when Jordan's phone rang. It was Heidi.

"Yes! Yes! Yes!" she screamed into the phone. Brian could hear the yells from the driver's seat. "Yes, I'll be your girlfriend. Have a great trip." And then Heidi hung up.

"What's up?" Brian asked as the car approached the passenger drop-off area.

"Looks like I've got a girlfriend," Jordan said with a huge smile.

It's All About Connections, Baby

Audrina

There were good days and bad days working at Quixote Studios, but the day Mike Collins came into Quixote was a day that would change Audrina's life.

As the receptionist of a busy production studio, Audrina met all types of people, some famous, some not so famous. Audrina would never forget the day George Clooney came in for a magazine cover shoot. Unlike many of the stars who passed through Quixote Studios, George didn't travel with an entourage. He just walked in on his own. This impressed Audrina. She felt he was making a statement by not needing a bunch of people with him everywhere he went. George stopped by Audrina's desk and chatted with her for a moment. Audrina didn't remember exactly what they talked about—her mind kind of went blank when faced with such movie-star hotness—but she did remember coming away with the idea that he was just as charming as she had imagined.

Even though she didn't recognize everyone who came into Quixote as easily as she did George Clooney, she did know that a lot of the people who were producing the cover shoots and videos might need other performers someday. So Audrina always made a point of getting to know the people who came in, especially the ones who returned often.

Mike Collins had never used Quixote Studios before, and his first day there producing a Dwight Yoakam video wasn't going exactly as planned. One of the girls they were planning to use in the video had called in sick, and Mike needed a new girl to replace her immediately.

"Excuse me, I'm Mike Collins. I'm producing the Dwight Yoakam video on stage three," he said, approaching Audrina's desk.

"Hello, Mr. Collins. I know who you are," said Audrina.

"Great. I've got a little problem, and I was hoping you could maybe help me out," he said.

"Sure, I'll see what I can do. What is it?"

"Well, one of the girls we're using for the video is sick."

"Do you need someone to take her home or to the hospital?" asked Audrina.

"No, no. Nothing like that. She didn't show, and I was wondering if maybe you could fill in. You act, don't you?" said Mike.

"Wow. Thank you. I do act, and it sounds really exciting. I'm just not allowed to leave my post for other work here at Quixote," said Audrina.

Mike was clearly disappointed. "You sure you can't, just this one time?" he pleaded.

"Sorry," Audrina said regretfully, hoping she wasn't missing out on her big break.

Mike paced in front of Audrina's desk, not sure what to do next.

Audrina mulled things over for a minute, then had an idea. "You know what, my friend Miranda might be available. She's been in videos before, and it's possible she's not working today," said Audrina.

"Call her, please. Does she live near here?" Mike said.

Newly energized with the possibility of Miranda coming, Mike focused on the clock above Audrina's desk. "I need her in an hour," he said.

Within moments Audrina was on the phone explaining it all to Miranda.

"She wants to talk to you," said Audrina as she handed Mike the telephone.

Mike took the phone. Audrina could tell it was all going to be OK. Miranda wasn't working that day and would love to come in

and help out Audrina. Mike hung up the phone, looking visibly relieved.

"Thanks, I owe you one. A big one. What's your name?" said Mike.

Audrina told him, and he wrote it down in his notebook. You never know what could happen when you help someone out in Hollywood.

Audrina's Favorite Celebrity Sightings at Quixote Studios

1. George Clooney

2. Rebecca Romijn

3. Johnny Depp

4. Britney Spears

5. Cindy Crawford

Ready for Her Close-Up

Audrina

Just a few weeks later, Audrina got a call at work from Mike. He was producing another video, this time for an up-and-coming band named PSOMA.

"We're shooting it on the weekend, and I'm hoping you'll be available to be in it," he said.

Audrina was speechless. Was she *available*? Was he joking?

"Of course," she blurted out.

Mike told her the particulars about where to show up: a warehouse in Hollywood, the time: seven A.M. (yikes!), and what she would be doing. Apparently, Audrina was going to be the lead girl in what would be a series of three videos. As Mike explained it, PSOMA was going to do a video trilogy featuring the same characters, similar to what Aerosmith had done in the nineties.

Audrina hung up the phone in disbelief. There were so many things to do before the shoot on Sunday. Her mind was reeling with all the doors this could open for her. The video would look great on her reel when she submitted it to agents and producers.

Clearly, the first thing to do, if she was going to be on film in four days, was to hit the gym to get her body into video vixen shape.

By Sunday morning Audrina felt she was close. She always worked out, but she'd really kicked it up a notch in the last four days, and her body was showing it. Audrina arrived at the Hollywood warehouse half an hour early. The production crew was setting up the space to shoot the video. The art director and her staff had transformed a huge empty warehouse to resemble a police station. It looked like something right out of *NYPD Blue*.

Audrina wandered around the set until she spotted Mike. He was happy to see her and gave her a hug hello.

"It's a beautiful set, isn't it?" he said.

"It looks great," Audrina said honestly.

"Audrina. Have I told you I love your name?" Mike asked.

"Uh, no, not really," she answered.

"Well, I do. Thanks for coming out so early. I know the money isn't great, but this is just the beginning," Mike said as they walked around the set.

Audrina would gladly have been in the video for free—but she didn't tell Mike that.

"We need you to get into hair and makeup, and then you can meet the band," Mike said.

He escorted Audrina over to the hairstylist, who immediately went to work on Audrina's hair. It took the stylist more than an hour to make Audrina's hair look exactly like it did when Audrina first woke up. If she had know that she had to look like a disaster, Audrina could have saved the stylist a lot of time and just come in that morning without washing or brushing her hair.

It turned out Audrina's character was supposed to look like she had been up all night partying. So with her hair a mess, Audrina next went to the makeup department, where the nice makeup guy made her look like she had spent a sleepless night drinking and crying. The black streaks of mascara running down her face looked incredibly authentic.

Mike was coming into the makeup room just as Audrina was leaving.

"You look great. Well, you look like crap, but that's great," Mike said.

"Thanks, I guess," Audrina said dryly.

"Let's go meet the guys."

The band was standing with their instruments in a room right next to the fake interrogation room. Mike introduced the four members of PSOMA to Audrina. She shook each of their hands, feeling a little self-conscious. It was her first time working with rock stars (well, hopefully they were soon-to-be rock stars), and she looked like a drowned rat. Great.

"I'm sorry I look so bad," she said nervously.

"You look great," they assured her.

Just then the director of the video came over and asked the

band to take their places. He introduced himself to Audrina and told her that she was going to be interrogated by an actor playing a detective.

The director went on to explain the character Audrina was playing and what he wanted from her. It was all happening so fast! Audrina could feel her heart racing, but she did her best to remain calm. She walked into the interrogation room and shook hands with the detective/actor, who said he was sorry he was going to be yelling at her during the filming. Audrina said it was fine; it was only make-believe, after all, and she was a professional—or was trying to be, at least.

The camera was set up; someone called for silence on the set.

"Roll film."

Then another person yelled, "Playback," and the song started playing.

The detective began yelling and screaming at Audrina. She'd never been so happy in her entire life.

Favorite Music

Audrina: AFI

Lauren: Death Cab For Cutie

Whitney: Mariah Carey

Heidi: Kelly Clarkson

Nothing Says Romance Like a Basket of Tacos

Whitney

Whitney's first college experience was at the University of Colorado at Boulder. Although she missed Southern California, and her family, too, she still found time to have a social life.

Alice, one of Whitney's friends, wanted to fix Whitney up with her brother, Cameron. Whitney was open to the idea, so Alice gave her brother Whitney's number. Cameron called Whitney, and they talked a bit, and then he asked her to dinner a few nights later.

The night of the date Whitney dressed with care, wanting to look her best. Cameron had said he was driving her all the way to Denver for dinner, so she was looking forward to going somewhere exciting. Soon the time Cameron was supposed to pick her up had come and gone. She got a call from Alice, who told Whitney to turn on her radio to a particular station. Whitney didn't understand what was going on, but she did as her friend asked and turned on the radio. To her surprise, after a few minutes she heard the guy she was supposed be on a date with talking to her on the radio. He must have gotten the DJ to let him send a broadcast message to Whitney.

"I just want to tell you I got a flat tire, but I'm almost on my way."

Whitney turned the radio off. It was kind of an odd way to let

her know that he was running late, but Whitney still was looking forward to the date. He finally showed an hour and a half later.

All the way to Denver, Whitney wondered where he was taking her.

When they pulled up outside of a Mexican fast-food chain, she couldn't believe it. Fast food? *Really?* She decided to be nice, though, and didn't express her disappointment to her date.

Unfortunately, the evening didn't improve from there. Whitney felt like she had to struggle to keep the conversation going or else there would be long awkward silences.

They made the long drive back to Boulder and said good night. A few weeks later Whitney decided to transfer to USC, to be closer to her family and to the city she loved. And when she reconnected with David, they did *not* spend their first date at a fast-food chain.

Turn-Offs

Lauren: Arrogance

Whitney: Condescension

Audrina: Guys who talk about ex-girlfriends

Heidi: Cockiness

Step Away from the Cardigans

Lauren and Heidi

After all the drama of finding an apartment in L.A., registering for classes at her new school, and landing the *Teen Vogue* internship, Lauren was ready to do some celebrating. And what better way to celebrate than shopping? She was definitely going to have to update her wardrobe if she wanted to shine for Lisa Love and everyone at *Teen Vogue*. There was clearly only one thing to do: She headed straight to Robertson.

Robertson Boulevard had the best stores for finding something cute, but sophisticated, to wear to work. Kitson, known for its fabulous selection and its even more fabulous clientele, was on Robertson. Paris, Nicole, Lindsay—they all shopped there.

Lisa Kline was across the street. Madison was on Robertson, too. It was hard to believe all those beautiful stores were right next to one another. And, if you wanted something to eat, The Ivy was there, too. It was two little blocks of shopping heaven.

Of course, shopping meant shopping with Heidi, since Heidi loved helping Lauren find the right clothes to wear, and that day was no different.

Their first stop was Madison. Heidi took the lead and peppered Lauren with questions: "What were the other girls wearing at the interview? Is it hot in the office? What kind of shoes did Lisa Love have on? Don't you love this skirt?"

Lauren replied in quick succession, "Mostly jeans. The office is cold. I didn't see her feet. No, it's got too many ruffles for me."

Heidi held up a black cotton cardigan sweater. "This would be good if the office is cold," she said.

Lauren was looking at a rack of skirts and didn't reply. Heidi found another black sweater, this one a bit longer with a roll collar.

"You're going to need a sweater," said Heidi.

"Is my mother here? Please, stop pushing the sweaters. I don't like them," replied Lauren.

Lauren moved over to a rack with tops, found one she liked, and instead of going over to the dressing room, just slipped the hanger over her head so she could see what the top would look like without having to try it on.

"That's nice," said Heidi.

"It's See by Chloé. It's Chloé's secondary line," Lauren said knowledgably.

Lauren liked the shirt, but she wasn't in love with it. And she had decided long ago not to buy anything she didn't absolutely adore. It was one of her most basic fashion rules.

She put the top back and walked over to an endless selection of pants, quickly finding three pairs she wanted to try on.

Meanwhile, Heidi was busy on the other side of the store, picking out four tops she thought Lauren would like. Breezing past the 5 ITEMS MAX PER ROOM sign, Lauren found a changing room and started trying on clothes.

The tops Heidi had picked out weren't really to Lauren's taste, but she tried one on anyway, for two reasons: One, she didn't want to hurt Heidi's feelings, and two, you never really knew what would look right until you tried it on anyway.

Lauren came out of the dressing room to show Heidi the new outfit.

"The top is all wrong, but I love those pants. They're really flattering. With some heels they'd be perfect," said Heidi.

They felt a little snug for Lauren's taste. Sensing her friend's trepidation, Heidi continued, "They're adorable. Very *Teen Vogue.*"

Lauren was swayed. They were indeed very *Teen Vogue*, and that was just what she needed right now.

It wasn't a complete outfit yet, but it was a good place to start. Both girls got a sense that they had seen everything in the store, so Lauren bought the pants, and they moved on.

Out on the sidewalk, Heidi seemed to be staring at Lauren, specifically, at her head.

"Is there something in my hair?" asked Lauren.

"No."

"Then why do you keep staring at it?" asked Lauren.

"I can't believe they want you to change your hair," said Heidi.

"I know. Blaine said the hair guy had something in mind for me," said Lauren.

"Like, if they said to me, 'We need to change your hair,' I'd be like, 'Really?' " said Heidi.

"I think they meant it more like, 'You don't have anything going on up there,' " said Lauren.

"I wonder if everyone has to go through it?"

"I don't know. I do have boring hair, so I'm not insulted," replied Lauren.

They had reached Sky, a great place for cute tops at decent prices. Lauren was immediately drawn to a rack of colorful tops. She found one she liked and held it up to show Heidi.

"I don't think so," Heidi said.

"These are more fun going-out tops," Lauren conceded.

"You know who has really cute clothes? Audrina. She always looks so good."

"I know. She's cute. I'm glad we met her," said Lauren.

"She's going out with a new guy tonight."

"She sure likes to go on dates," Lauren observed. She held up another top for Heidi's inspection.

"That would work good with a sweater, but I'm dropping the sweaters, no more mentioning the evil sweaters. Good-bye, cardigans, good-bye, V-necks, good-bye to anything that looks like it's knitted," Heidi said playfully.

And so it went. A shopping girl's work was never done—at least until it was time to stop for lunch.

Fashion Favorites

Lauren: Marc Jacobs

Whitney: John Galliano

Audrina: Betsey Johnson

Heidi: Chanel

Highlights Make Everything Better

Lauren and Whitney

Wearing her new pants and a top she'd finally found that she liked, Lauren walked into the exclusive Neil George Salon, which has a huge celebrity clientele, and gave the girl behind the counter her name. The girl said that Justin, her hairstylist, would be right with her, but first she had to change into a smock. After Lauren put on the cover-up, Justin came over and introduced himself.

"Now, who sent you in today?" Justin asked.

"Lisa Love," answered Lauren. "I got an internship."

"Oh, really. Exciting. She sends all the girls in here," said Justin.

Lauren was relieved to know that she wasn't the first person to be sent over to get her hair changed. Justin escorted Lauren over to his chair, then circled behind her, evaluating her hair.

"We're just going to change up your look a bit," he said.

Lauren was fine with that. Justin ran his fingers through different parts of her hair.

"I think we'll bring a little more of your natural color out. We'll tone out some of these ends. Add a few lowlights underneath, so it looks more natural and so the lighter pieces are on the ends. Then we'll go from the top and rehighlight it. Does that sound cool?"

Did that sound cool? That sounded fantastic!

"Yes, that would be great," Lauren replied, barely able to hide her excitement.

"So, do you know how many days you'll be working?" asked Justin.

"No, they haven't really told me anything yet," said Lauren. And then she saw Whitney walk into the salon. She felt a wave of relief that Whitney, too, was going to be getting a hair update.

Whitney sat down in the chair next to Lauren.

"Did Blaine call you?" asked Lauren.

"Yeah, he said my hair was overprocessed and too surfer girl," said Whitney.

"Blaine told me my hair was too Orange County," confided Lauren.

"Ouch."

"It's OK, I was totally down to change my hair," said Lauren.

Whitney nodded, and the counter girl took her to put on a cover-up. Justin combed Lauren's hair into different sections, getting it ready for all the treatments.

"Did you have to buy a whole new wardrobe for your new job?" he asked.

"I found a couple of things yesterday. These pants are new," said Lauren.

"Well, they look beautiful on you," said Justin.

Lauren thanked Justin for the compliment. Just then, Whitney came back and sat down, now appropriately covered and ready for her own hair makeover.

Justin asked, "Did they say anything to you about what you were supposed to wear?"

"They didn't tell me anything," said Whitney.

"I guess we'll find out," added Lauren.

Justin continued with Lauren's hair as his assistant started working on Whitney's blond mane. Justin had one more question for them. "Are you guys nervous about working at *Teen Vogue*?"

"A little," both girls said at once.

The girls blushed and smiled at each other. They didn't know it yet, but the internship was going to be a great experience for them both.

They Say Poor Penmanship Is a Sign of Genius

Lauren and Whitney

Lauren and Whitney's first day at *Teen Vogue* consisted mainly of addressing invitations and stuffing envelopes for the magazine's upcoming Young Hollywood Party. At one point Olivia, the fashion stylist, came into the room where the girls were working and gave each of them some unsolicited fashion advice. She even accused Whitney of being too matchy-matchy! Lauren and Whitney didn't quite know what to make of it.

But they didn't have time to dwell on it, because there was work to be done. Whitney and Lauren started addressing the envelopes. There were stacks and stacks of them. Lauren was addressing envelopes to every celebrity in town. She couldn't believe it. Heidi would be so jealous! Lauren had to call her. She got out her cell phone and quickly dialed Heidi's number.

"You're not going to believe who I'm addressing an invitation to," Lauren said as a greeting.

"One of those hobbit guys," Heidi guessed.

"No, it's . . ." Lauren stopped talking as Lisa Love walked into the intern closet. Lauren dropped the cell and prayed that Lisa hadn't seen her on the phone.

Lisa asked to see a sample of each of the girls' envelopes. When Lauren handed over an envelope she had addressed, she could sense Lisa's disapproval. Lauren wasn't sure if the look on Lisa's face was because of the phone call or because of her handwriting.

"From here on out, why don't we have Whitney address all the envelopes, and Lauren, you can seal them and add the postage," said Lisa.

"OK," said Lauren.

As quickly as Lisa Love had arrived, she left. Whitney looked over at Lauren. "Sorry," she said sheepishly.

"That's OK. I haven't done cursive since, like, the fourth grade," Lauren replied. She picked up her phone again, to discover that Heidi had hung up on her. She pressed redial.

"So, who were you writing an invitation to?" Heidi asked when she answered the phone.

"Hayden Christensen," replied Lauren.

"No way!"

Lauren grinned. She didn't really get celebrity crushes herself, so she found Heidi's fangirlishness extremely amusing. "You wouldn't believe some of the names on this list. I haven't even heard of some of the people."

"That is so cool," said Heidi.

"Oh my god, this morning, this stylist came in and reaccessorized our outfits without us asking her to," said Lauren. "She came in and was like, 'Let me look at your *ensemble.*' "

"I didn't even know you *had* an ensemble," quipped Heidi.

"I know, right? While she's doing it, all I'm thinking is, *Are you seriously changing my clothes?* Now I'm going to be super self-conscious about everything I wear here," said Lauren.

"That's awful, Lauren."

"I gotta go."

Lauren closed her phone and started licking envelopes. After the first one she sighed and thought, *Only 499 more to go.*

Bombs Away

Audrina

It was a busy day at Quixote Studios. There were big shoots happening on all three stages. One was a commercial for Verizon and the other two were magazine cover shoots, one for *Playboy* and the other for *Entertainment Weekly*. As usual, the phones had been going crazy, and Audrina barely had a free moment. Answering the phones was an important part of her job—she was essentially "the voice" of Quixote Studios—but some days, it was a lot to juggle. On the slower days, she would be able to walk around and see what was happening on each stage and meet the people who were working there. But this definitely wasn't one of those days. So when a guy introducing himself as Nick came up to her desk to ask which way to stage two, and there were three different phone lines ringing, it was possible Audrina came off as rude in her response, because she just pointed down the hallway.

Nick headed to the stage but was back a few minutes later, looking for the craft services table this time. Since he had just walked right by it, all piled high with snacks, Audrina suspected he was coming back to her desk for another reason. She sent him off in the right direction, curious to see what would happen next.

Sure enough, Nick kept finding reasons to come back throughout the day, with a question or request for directions, and at the end of the day he asked for her phone number. Audrina thought Nick was cute, and she liked the attention he had shown her that day, so she gave it to him.

It was barely twenty-four hours later when Nick called and asked her if she'd like to go out to dinner at Blowfish Sushi. Audrina loved sushi. She wasn't sure if she had told Nick that fact or not. So, either he was attentive and listened, or it was just good luck. Either way, Audrina was happy to say yes.

The night of their date, Audrina waited at her apartment for the doorbell to ring. This waiting-around-after-you-were-ready-to-go-out was the hardest part. She just wanted the date to start, and Nick was running a little late according to her watch.

Finally, the doorbell rang. Audrina waited a minute before she answered, so he wouldn't think she was just waiting around for him.

"Hi, you ready to go?" Nick said with a smile.

"I just got home from work," Audrina fibbed, "but yeah, I can't wait."

In the parking lot downstairs, Nick held the car door open for her. Audrina thought, *This might be the start of a good date.*

As they drove out of the parking lot, Audrina asked, "What did you do today?"

"I quit," Nick said.

"Really?"

"Yeah."

"What are you going to do?" Audrina asked.

"I just quit for the day. So, I'll go back tomorrow," Nick said.

Oh-kay. Maybe this wasn't going to be a good date after all. Only time would tell.

They arrived at Blowfish Sushi and were seated by the hostess. When the waiter came over to take their drink orders, Audrina ordered an Arnold Palmer and Nick asked for a large sake and a Sapporo. As they waited for the drinks, an uncomfortable silence descended. What had looked like a promising night just a few minutes ago now seemed to be on the downward slide toward boring.

The drinks arrived, and Audrina gratefully sipped her Arnold Palmer.

"Have you ever done a sake bomb?" Nick asked.

"What are those?" replied Audrina.

"It's when you put your chopsticks across the top of your glass like this," Nick explained, as he moved his chopsticks to rest on the rim of his beer.

"Then you put your shot glass of sake on top of the chopsticks," he said, doing just that.

"Then you pound on the table and the shot of sake falls into the beer, and then you chug."

Nick hadn't pounded on the table yet so his sake was still waiting on top of the beer. Audrina didn't say anything; she just looked at Nick, not quite believing what he was doing.

"What drink did you get?" he asked.

Audrina stifled a sigh. Nick wasn't turning out to be the observant interested guy she thought he would be. "I got an Arnold Palmer," she said.

"What's that?"

"It's half iced tea, half lemonade. Would you like some?" Audrina said.

"I thought it was a *drink* drink. Want to try a sake bomb?" he asked.

Audrina thought about it, but not for long. She really had nothing to lose. It certainly couldn't make the evening go any worse.

"Sure. Set me up," she said.

Nick poured Audrina a big glass of beer, placed the chopsticks across the rim, and set the shot glass of sake on top of that.

"Now we pound the table at the same time," said Nick.

Nick and Audrina each slammed the side of their fists on the table, knocking the sake glasses into the waiting beer. Now the challenge was to drink the bubbling mixture quickly. Nick was already halfway through his sake bomb as Audrina brought the glass to her lips. She drank as much as she could and then set the glass back down on the table. She noticed that Nick had finished his entire glass. Big surprise.

Now it was Nick's turn to look disappointed.

"You didn't even finish," he said.

"I can't drink that fast," she said defensively.

"And you didn't say, 'Sake bomb.' "

"I didn't know you had to say, 'Sake bomb,'" Audrina replied. Was he serious?

"Well, we better go again," Nick said.

Audrina wasn't about to let this Nick character show her up as a novice drinker. They lined up the drinks again.

Three sake bombs into the night and the date seemed to be going a bit better. At least they were both happy.

Somehow the discussion turned to old boyfriends.

"So when was your last long-term relationship?" Nick asked.

"It's been a while," said Audrina.

"It's been a while for me, too," he said. "I had this one girlfriend; I had a really hard time breaking up with her."

Audrina was trying to figure out where this conversation was going, but she had started feeling the full effect of the sake bombs.

"Do you know my friend Brian?" she asked suddenly.

"Who's he?"

"He's just a guy who lives with Heidi's boyfriend," Audrina explained.

"You like him or something?" Nick asked suspiciously.

"Brian? No. He's just a funny guy. I thought you knew him for some reason," Audrina said.

"No, I don't know any funny guys named Brian."

Audrina shrugged and looked around the restaurant. She

spotted a guy she knew from work at another table. He waved to her, and Audrina waved back.

"You don't get jealous, do you?" Nick asked.

"I don't get jealous very easily," Audrina said.

"I get jealous real easily," Nick said.

"I was just waving to a guy I work with," Audrina said defensively.

Even though Nick was doing almost everything wrong, Audrina had to admit she was still attracted to him. Sometimes you just don't go for the guys who are good for you. Audrina knew that better than anyone.

Dating 101:
What Your Mom Didn't Tell You

Audrina: Pretty boys are nice to hang out with, but they're boring.

Heidi: The perk of dating a model: You're dating a great physique.

Lauren: Flowers mean "I'm sorry"; chocolates mean "I love you."

Whitney: Great conversation is all you need for a great date.

Divalicious

Brian

Brian didn't mind dressing up in women's clothes. He had done it before, for auditions, and had dressed as Britney Spears for a Halloween party. There was nothing really strange about it. The only strange thing was other people's reactions. But today Brian was dressing up as a woman for work.

After a grueling audition process, Brian had been cast in a movie called *Iron Man*, playing a transvestite, and he couldn't be happier about the opportunity, no matter what he had to wear.

Audrina and Brian hamming it up at a Halloween party.

Early Wednesday morning, Brian walked into the makeup room at the studio.

"My sister always said I looked like a girl," he told the makeup woman to crack the ice.

The woman laughed as she continued to apply his makeup. Brian felt a rush of excitement. This was the first day of shooting for Brian on his first real movie.

What was making it an extra-special day was that Brian's dad was going to be joining him on the set. His dad lived in Florida, but he had just arrived in L.A. to visit his son.

As Brian was getting his makeup done, he continued cracking jokes with the makeup artist. Brian wondered why more men didn't wear makeup and he wanted to know if he would be more attractive with collagen injected in his lips. By the time the makeup and false eyelashes had been applied, Brian was impressed by how much he looked like a woman.

"I think my voice is still too low, though," he quipped.

The wardrobe department put Brian in a sequined midriff-baring top, a short skirt, and a yellow feather boa. Brian loved it. Then his dad showed up. Brian's father walked into the wardrobe room and said, "I used to have a son and a daughter; now I've got two daughters."

Brian's scene was coming up, so he was called to the set; his dad went with him. Brian introduced his father to the director and producer, and then his dad stood off to one side so as not to be in anyone's way.

Brian's scene was about trying to convince another actor that he wasn't a guy. Unfortunately, the other actor kept screwing up the lines. Brian glanced at his dad between takes. He was having one of the most exciting days of his life, and he loved that his father was there to share it with him.

The other actor finally figured out his lines, and they did the scene again. This time everything went smoothly. After the director yelled, "Cut," Brian's dad came over and gave Brian a huge bear hug.

"I'm so proud of you," he said.

Brian had never felt better in his life, and so what if he was dressed as a woman? He was an actor, and actors had to do crazy stuff sometimes. It was all part of the job.

"You'll do great at this, Brian. Just don't ask to keep the wardrobe," said his dad.

Covering for Your Roommate 101

Lauren

Although Heidi had followed Lauren to Los Angeles to go to fashion school, now that Heidi was taking a job with Bolthouse Productions, she decided to drop out of school. Lauren would have to go to classes on her own. It didn't exactly upset Lauren, but it didn't make her feel all warm and fuzzy toward Heidi, either.

Lauren drove her BMW into the school parking lot and settled for a spot on the far side. Although she was on time, the lot was already three quarters full. Lauren loved the days when she pulled into the lot and there was a primo parking spot waiting for her; it made her feel like the rest of day was going to go her way, too. Clearly that wasn't the case this morning. Instead she felt like she'd have to be on the lookout the rest of the day for anything bad on the horizon.

She got out of the car, slung two black school bags over her shoulders, and headed across the street to the FIDM campus. As she was crossing the quad in front of the main building, out of the corner of her eye, she spotted Susan Aronson, her counselor. Any other day, Lauren would have liked bumping into Susan, but not today. Lauren knew Susan would ask her about Heidi, and Lauren didn't have an answer prepared, and it annoyed her that she even felt like she should. From across the lawn Susan had seen Lauren, too. Now Lauren would have to stop and say something. Any other course of action would be rude, and she didn't need to piss off anybody this early in the quarter.

Lauren steeled herself and walked up the small grassy knoll to say hello to Susan.

"I heard through the grapevine that you got the *Teen Vogue* internship. Congratulations," Susan said.

"Thank you," Lauren said.

"So, how is it going?" Susan pressed.

"It's a good internship; I like it a lot," Lauren said.

"And how is school treating you so far?" Susan asked.

"Good," Lauren said.

"It's a lot to juggle. A lot to balance. I want you to know I'm here for you, if you have any questions," Susan said.

"Thanks."

Lauren could tell Susan was about to end the conversation, which was fine with her. She wanted to get to class and avoid having to talk about Heidi. Lauren was pretty sure her roommate hadn't called the school to say she was dropping out. And then, just as Susan was taking her first step away from Lauren, she looked back and said, "I thought I'd see you walking down with Heidi. Where is she today?"

Lauren didn't want to lie, but she also didn't want to get into a big thing about Heidi dropping out, especially after Susan had been so nice to Heidi.

"I don't know where she is today," Lauren said truthfully.

"Well, I hope everything's going well for her," Susan said.

"She's fine," Lauren responded.

As Lauren continued on her way to class, she couldn't help but wish that Heidi would take more responsibility for her actions. It was becoming more and more obvious that living with Heidi wasn't exactly what Lauren had thought it would be.

Rules of Engagement

Heidi and Audrina

Heidi had known Audrina for a couple of months, but still hadn't seen her apartment. Audrina had visited Heidi and Lauren's place, but never the other way around. That was finally changing tonight. Audrina really wanted to talk to Heidi about something, and she didn't want to do it over the phone. So before dinner, Heidi walked over to Audrina's apartment. The journey took all of three minutes.

"Oh my gosh, what a pretty home," Heidi said as she entered. "I totally like your apartment. It's super cozy. Kinda girly."

"Girly—I guess that's a good thing," Audrina said.

Heidi pointed at a half-painted purple wall. "What happened over there?"

"I still have to finish painting that," Audrina said sheepishly.

Audrina and Heidi moved to the living room area. Heidi sat down on the couch, and Audrina took the love seat.

Audrina spilled her news, the reason she had asked Heidi to come over to talk. "Brian was drunk the other night, the night of the *Teen Vogue* party that Lauren was working. I brought him home with me."

"You brought Brian home? Audrina, I had no idea!" said Heidi, genuinely surprised.

"Nothing happened," Audrina said quickly. "He curled up in front of the fireplace and went to sleep."

"Oh my gosh, right over there? It looks uncomfortable," said Heidi, wrinkling her nose.

"He was too busy passing out to complain," said Audrina.

"Why'd he sleep on the floor instead of the couch?"

"You'd have to ask Brian," Audrina said with a laugh.

"What did he say in the morning?" asked Heidi.

"Nothing. I got up, showered, had breakfast, and left for work. He was still asleep when I left, and he was gone when I came home," said Audrina.

"That Brian's a funny guy," said Heidi. She liked Brian; he was nice enough and, of course, he was Jordan's roommate. But falling asleep in front of Audrina's fireplace wasn't the way to impress a girl. Heidi knew Brian had a little crush on Audrina—he'd recently asked Heidi if he had a shot at going out with her.

"So what's up with you and Nick?" Heidi asked, trying to get the lay of the land.

"I'm still talking to him," said Audrina.

"How did your date go?"

"OK, I guess. He seemed like the jealous type," said Audrina. She shifted in the love seat. "Have you ever done sake bombs?"

"No. Is that some sort of drink?" asked Heidi.

Audrina explained what it was and how she had had three of them on her date.

"Did you mention Brian to Nick?" Heidi asked.

"Yeah, but so what?" Audrina said.

"Oh my god, Audrina, no wonder he was jealous. You don't tell a guy about another guy; that's, like, player rule number one," said Heidi.

Heidi knew now was the moment to give a plug for Brian. But what could she say that would make him still seem desirable?

"I don't think Brian's the jealous type," she ventured.

Okay, that alone probably wasn't going to do the trick. She needed to think of something better—something, anything.

"You know, Brian's doing stand-up in a few weeks, and I know he'd really like to see you there," Heidi said coyly.

Audrina thought about it for a moment.

"That sounds like it might be fun," she said.

Heidi beamed triumphantly. Heidi the matchmaker had struck again.

Heidi's Other Player Rules

1. Don't hate the player, hate the game.

2. Actually, don't hate the game, either.

3. Celebrities are always attractive.

4. Don't date anyone unattractive, unless they're a celebrity.

Honky-tonk Dreams

Jordan

Now that Jordan was settled in Los Angeles, he really wanted to pursue becoming a country-and-western singer. Brian would become an actor and Jordan would become a singer—that was the plan. But then Heidi happened. Jordan didn't realize that having a girlfriend would take up so much of his time. All the energy he had intended to put into his music, he put into his relationship instead. Brian teased him about it sometimes, but Jordan just couldn't find the energy to do both.

That all changed after Jordan and Heidi got into an argument in which Heidi accused him of not following his dreams. The accusation hurt—especially since he knew there was some truth to it—and he realized it was time to get up off his butt and do something. He called up the Musicians Institute and booked a session with their best vocal coach. But when Jordan hung up the phone, he began to wonder if he had done the right thing. He started getting nervous and he didn't know why.

Jordan had made the appointment with a guy named Hacksaw—not the name you'd expect to be attached to a vocal coach. But Jordan had heard about Hacksaw from a few friends, and they all swore by him. That didn't stop Jordan from being a ball of nerves.

As if Hacksaw's name wasn't intimidating enough, when Jordan entered the classroom at MI, he found out that Hacksaw stood well over six feet tall. Either he sensed Jordan's nervousness, or everyone was nervous before their first session, because Hacksaw did his best to make Jordan feel at ease.

First he asked about Jordan's previous singing experience. Jordan had had singing lessons before, and he had sung in the church choir back home. But this was a totally different type of singing. Hacksaw ran his fingers along the keyboard and hit a note. He asked Jordan to sing it.

"Not bad, not bad at all," said Hacksaw.

Hacksaw hit more notes, and Jordan sang the notes perfectly. Then they moved on to scales. Hacksaw played them, and Jordan sang them. Soon Jordan was feeling a bit more at ease and started enjoying himself. His passion for singing was returning, and he had the argument with Heidi to thank for it.

The lesson ended with Jordan thanking Hacksaw profusely and telling him that he would be back again for sure.

At the apartment that night, Jordan gave Heidi a hug and a kiss the minute she walked into the apartment.

"What was that for?" Heidi asked.

"For telling me to follow my dreams," Jordan said.

Jordan explained how great the session had gone and how nervous he had been before he went without knowing why. But then Heidi explained it all for him.

"You were nervous because this is important to you. If you took that singing lesson and found out you sucked, that your dreams weren't going to come true, that would have been awful. And part of you knew you could do it and another part of you doubted it. That's all it was," said Heidi.

"Thanks, doctor," Jordan said teasingly.

"So what did you make us for dinner?" Heidi asked.

"We're going out tonight," said Jordan.

And so Jordan took Heidi out to dinner at her favorite sushi restaurant and thanked her all night long.

The Little Single Lovebird

Lauren, Heidi, and Jordan

It was morning in West Hollywood, and Heidi and Jordan were soaking up the rays by the pool. Heidi thought that she could get used to this no-school stuff, even though her job at Bolthouse Productions would start in a few days. She figured that her work schedule at Bolthouse would still leave her plenty of time to hang out by the pool with her boyfriend.

"I want to play all day," Heidi said.

"Don't we already play all day?" Jordan said.

"Yeah, I just want to stay *here* all day," she clarified.

"We could do that."

Without school to break up her day, Heidi was looking at a long stream of uninterrupted daylight hours with almost no responsibilities at all. That was the kind of lifestyle she could embrace. As Heidi soaked up the sun, Jordan interrupted her thoughts.

"Where's Audrina? Wanna do something with her today?" he asked.

"She's at work," Heidi said without looking up.

"She's always at work," said Jordan.

"Some people have to work, Jordan Patrick Eubanks," said Heidi. She liked to use Jordan's full name when reprimanding him.

"Work sucks," Jordan declared.

"So you've said before."

And so the day went. Heidi and Jordan lounged by the pool

talking about their less fortunate friends who had to go to an office and spend all day inside.

"Let's go on a date. Dinner and a movie," said Jordan.

"A matinee. Lunch and a movie. I love movies in the middle of the day," said Heidi.

Just as they were about to solidify their plans, Lauren entered the pool area with two book bags on her shoulders. Lauren walked over to the sunbathers.

"Look how cute you are," Heidi said.

"Where are you going?" Jordan asked.

Heidi knew full well where Lauren was going and wished that Jordan had not brought it up. She didn't like hearing any mention of school now that she had dropped out.

"Going to school. I've got a big test," Lauren said, and then added, "What are you guys doing?"

"Nothing," Heidi said, stating the obvious. She was glad that Lauren didn't bring up the fact that Heidi had dropped out. She felt bad about leaving her roommate to go to school alone, but Bolthouse was an opportunity she couldn't pass up. Would Lauren turn down Marc Jacobs if he offered her a job? Heidi didn't think so. Ultimately, Heidi had to do what was right for Heidi.

"Do you want to go out with us tonight?" Jordan asked.

"Yeah, just the three of us," Heidi said.

"You can be our 'third wheel,' " Jordan added.

"That sounds good," Lauren said. "I'm like that little birdie in that commercial. In the commercial there were all these little couple birds paired off. And there was, like, one little bird by himself, and he's like, 'It's cool. I had plans anyways.' I'm the little bird."

"Not for long," Heidi said.

"It's okay. I like being the little single lovebird. I gotta go. See you guys later."

"I'll call you later," said Heidi, as Lauren walked off.

Heidi could tell that even though Lauren put on a brave face, she was getting sick of being the third wheel. Who wouldn't?

As the day stretched out before them, Jordan leaned over and whispered, "Can we make out now?"

This is the life, Heidi thought. Lounging poolside in the middle of the day with nothing to do but kiss. "Of course," she said.

Dirty Laundry

Heidi and Jordan

It had been a long day at Bolthouse Productions and Heidi was looking forward to just going home and relaxing with Jordan. She had called him from the car on her way home, and he said he was doing laundry, which made her happy. Even though Jordan had his own apartment, he spent most of his time at his girlfriend's place, mostly because he could see more of Heidi that way and because her apartment was cleaner.

Heidi opened the door to the apartment.

"Hey, baby," she said to Jordan, who was lounging on the couch. Heidi walked over, gave Jordan a hug, and sat down beside him.

"What'd you do all day?" Heidi asked.

"I slept. I feel a little run-down still," he said. He had been sick recently and wasn't yet a hundred percent.

Jordan was moving around on the couch as if Heidi had invaded his space. She playfully moved closer to him, and he squirmed.

"I miss you all day, and you don't want to play," she pouted.

"You leave me all day and make me mad. By the time you get home, I'm mad at you," Jordan said.

Heidi responded with a smile; she knew Jordan didn't really mean what he said. She hugged him tighter.

"Come on; love on me," she said, wanting her snuggling to be reciprocated.

Jordan gave her a little hug and asked what work had been like. She explained that it had been a slow day.

"It seems like you're always talking to me on instant messenger or you're on the Internet. I'd like to sit there and get paid to do nothing," Jordan grumbled.

Heidi wasn't sure why Jordan was acting this way. She leaned over and looked into her bedroom.

"Did you do the laundry, baby?" she asked.

"No, baby."

"You said you were doing it," Heidi said, her voice getting a bit louder.

"I'm organizing it," Jordan replied, on the defensive.

Heidi got up and went into the bedroom to have a closer look. She was surprised to see all of her clothes and all of Jordan's clothes in big loose piles all around the room.

"It looks like a tornado in here," she said.

From the couch Jordan said, "I'm in the process."

"Of what, a tornado?" Heidi snapped.

Jordan laid his head back on the couch and let out a small moan. "I'm sorry, baby, I'm really tired," he said.

Heidi came out of the bedroom and gave Jordan another hug and said, "I know, you had a tough day."

Jordan didn't know if she was teasing him or not. But it didn't matter; Heidi was home and they could finally hang out, just like Jordan had wanted to do all day.

The Glamorous Life of Interns

Lauren and Whitney

Lauren and Whitney were in the process of finding reference photographs for an upcoming cover shoot and looking through head shots to find the right models for the next issue. Lauren was sitting on the floor going through the head shots, and Whitney was at her computer researching reference photos. The entire office was abuzz with activity. Lauren had never experienced anything quite like it. With everyone rushing to close the issue and get it off to the printer, it seemed as if they were moving at twice their normal speed.

Blaine, who they'd barely seen all day, rushed into the room, out of breath.

"We need all these clothes," he said, pointing to four enormous boxes stacked near Lauren, "unpacked, steamed, and racked. And Lisa would like you girls to make a coffee run." Then he disappeared down the hall.

Lauren looked at Whitney. "Well, I guess we better go get the coffee order going."

Whitney grabbed a small pad of paper and a pencil, and then they went around to all the editors' offices to take their orders. Getting coffee at *Teen Vogue* was a big deal. There was usually one run in the morning around 10:30 A.M. and then another in the afternoon around 3:30 P.M. The interns or one of the assistants would take the order and then go around the corner to The Coffee Bean & Tea Leaf. There was a coffee place on the main floor of the *Teen Vogue* building, but their java didn't measure up. It had to be The Coffee Bean.

There were twelve orders in all that day. One person couldn't carry that many coffees—Lauren had found that out the hard way her first week at the magazine—so hopefully today they had enough intern power to make it back upstairs safely with all twelve coffees intact. Lauren had her doubts.

"How are we going to carry all of them?" she asked Whitney.

"I'm guessing trays," Whitney replied.

"I can always count on you to know that kind of intern-y stuff," Lauren said with a grin.

Whitney gets the latest scoop from *Teen Vogue.*

As they walked into The Coffee Bean, Whitney said, "Smells delish." Both girls liked escaping the office during the day, even if it was just to get coffee. The guy at the counter recognized them and said hello. Whitney pulled out the sheet and handed it over to him. With Whitney's neat handwriting, they had found it was easier to just hand the list over rather than saying the order. It also allowed for one less misinterpretation of the order, and that, too, was a good thing—one less chance for them to get in trouble.

The girls found some vacant chairs and had a seat as the order was prepared.

"So, are things going good with that guy?" Lauren asked.

"David," Whitney said.

"Right. Besides David, you don't have any other ones?" Lauren said.

"No. One is fine for me," replied Whitney.

"Seriously? In a school with so many boys?"

"It's true. What about you?" said Whitney.

"Nobody right now," said Lauren.

"You spend a lot of time with Heidi and Jordan, right?"

"Yeah, Heidi and Jordan are, like, always together. I'm their third wheel," said Lauren.

Before Whitney could reply, the coffees were ready. Three trays, with four coffees in each tray.

Lauren took two trays, and Whitney just the one. Last time they had done a coffee run, Lauren was the lucky girl who only had to carry one tray. They traded off each time, and that seemed to work well.

It was a little precarious for Lauren, but the girls managed to make it into the elevator without spilling a drop. Whitney was going over the list one last time to make sure they had everybody's order right. It all looked good. The elevator doors opened, and Whitney stepped out first. As Lauren was stepping out of the elevator, her left foot hit the crack between the elevator and the floor, causing the top tray of coffee to jump out of her hands. For a moment, Lauren thought it was all over. The coffee would hit the ground, and then she would have to clean it up and then go downstairs and replace the order, and they would probably fire her, too. But miraculously, Whitney moved in just in time to catch the tray in midair and save the coffee from crashing to the floor.

"Oh my god, how did you do that?" Lauren said.

"I don't know," Whitney said, surprised at her own skill.

"Thank you so, so much," Lauren said.

The girls delivered the coffee without further incident. Then it was time to unload clothes and steam them. An intern's work was never done.

The Key to Love

Lauren and Jason

Lauren and Jason, her boyfriend from Laguna Beach, were finally back together and hitting the L.A. nightlife as much as possible. Tonight was Friday night, which meant Lauren and Jason were going to Basque, a club in Hollywood. It had taken Lauren a little while to figure out Los Angeles and how different clubs operated on different nights, but now that she had the hang of things, Friday night meant Basque. (One thing Lauren and Jason both liked about living in Los Angeles was the fact that you could do just about anything you wanted at night, unlike the small-town life of Laguna Beach.)

Jason had surprised Lauren that evening by cooking her dinner. "I just opened a can of soup and made some sandwiches," he said when Lauren thanked him, not wanting to make a big deal out of it. Lauren didn't push it. Sometimes Jason would just do nice things for her, and she was happy with that.

Lauren had come home from her internship later than expected, but Jason had been kind enough to keep the soup warm. Heidi and Jordan weren't around that Friday evening. Heidi had said something about staying at Jordan's place for the weekend. Lauren had to admit it was fun having the apartment to herself. She could eat whenever and whatever she wanted and she didn't have to clean up all the time. On the other hand, it meant there was never any food in the house and everything was always kind of messy. Lauren saw it as a trade-off.

After dinner Lauren changed into her outfit for the evening. When the sun was up Lauren preferred lighter-colored skirts and tops, paired with casual flats or flip-flops. At night she leaned more toward dark tops and even darker jeans, accented with high heels. She switched handbags, too, transferring her money and phone to the smaller bag.

Jason, for his part, didn't bother changing; he just added a jacket to his ensemble and was ready to go.

They didn't have any trouble getting into the club, since both Jason and Lauren knew the guy at the door. Jason really didn't like standing in line and he usually made sure if they were going out that he knew the promoter or whoever would be working the door that night.

Inside Basque it was hot and loud. Lauren saw a couple of

girls she knew from Laguna and chatted with them for a while. They were a few years ahead of Lauren in school and were currently attending UCLA. Lauren told them all about FIDM and the *Teen Vogue* internship. In the VIP section they spotted Nicky Hilton and Kevin Connolly, an actor from *Entourage* who was also Nicky's boyfriend. The Laguna girls apparently had some connection to Nicky, so they left Lauren to go say hi to the hotel heiress.

The rest of the night Jason and Lauren had fun running into friends and dancing nonstop. They would go out on the dance floor for hours. There was an exciting feeling in the club that night and Lauren didn't want the night to end. But the club had to close eventually, and at the end of the night Lauren and Jason headed back to Lauren's apartment.

By the time they got to the apartment complex it was almost three in the morning. As Lauren was feeling around her bag for the key she was thinking how glad she was that she didn't have work or school the next day. As her hand rooted around the inside of the handbag, Lauren had another feeling, that sinking feeling one has when impending doom comes into focus.

"I don't think I have the key," Lauren said.

"Seriously?"

"Yeah, seriously."

Lauren dumped out the contents of her handbag on the hallway carpet. Jason checked his own pockets just to make sure he hadn't grabbed the key before they left.

"It's not here," Lauren said.

"I guess we'll have to wake Heidi up," Jason said, as he pressed the doorbell.

"She's staying at Jordan's tonight," Lauren said.

Lauren sat down on the carpet outside her front door.

"What do you want to do?" Jason said.

Lauren had no idea. They didn't have an extra key hidden

anywhere, because there was nowhere to hide a key in the apartment hallway.

"Does Audrina have a key to your apartment?" Jason asked.

Heidi and Lauren had talked about getting extra keys made and giving one to Audrina, but they hadn't gotten around to it yet. Jason suggested they go to his place, but then remembered it was getting painted and everything was covered and smelled of paint.

"I've got it. We get back in the car and head over to Jordan's and get Heidi's key," Jason said.

It wasn't such a bad idea. Heidi and Jordan would probably be annoyed, but Lauren and Jason needed to sleep. On the way over to Jordan's place Jason said he would handle everything. Lauren was grateful Jason was there to help her out. She was so tired that she fell asleep in the car on the way.

Jason didn't want to wake Lauren, so he left her in the car when he went upstairs to get the key from Heidi. Jason rang the doorbell. Jordan answered the door quickly, like he hadn't been asleep.

"What's up?" Jordan asked.

"Nothing, I just wanted to come by and say hi," Jason fibbed.

As Jason had suspected, Jordan hadn't been sleeping. He was up playing *Madden Football* on his PlayStation.

"Where's Heidi?" Jason asked.

"She went to sleep hours ago," Jordan explained.

Jason asked if he could see Heidi's purse. Jordan said it was on the counter in the kitchen.

"Did you come here at three in the morning to borrow money?" Jordan asked as Jason went through Heidi's purse. Jason found the keys and held them up for Jordan to see.

"Oh, I get it now," Jordan said.

Jason thanked Jordan and said good-bye, then went back to the car where Lauren was still sleeping.

At the Hillside Villas, Jason gently woke Lauren and walked her to the apartment, then unlocked the door with Heidi's key. Lauren had never been so happy to be home in her own bed.

The next morning, Lauren got up and made Jason breakfast in bed as a thank you for dealing with last night's lost key, grateful to have a thoughtful and loving boyfriend who helped out when life took a weird turn.

Later that day Lauren and Jason went to the key-making hut in the Grove and had three extra keys made. Jason got one, Audrina got one, and Lauren put the last one in her car, so that she would never be locked out of her apartment again.

He Might as Well Be Dead

Audrina

Even after their odd dinner at Blowfish, Audrina was still attracted to Nick. He was kind of compact, just about Audrina's height, and his arms were completely tatted up. Not that height and tattoos alone were reasons to like a guy, but they were two things that appealed to Audrina's sense of what was sexy. She loved that rock-and-roll look.

So she and Nick had gone out on a few more dates, each weirder than the next. Nick seemed to have a habit of lying quite a bit. He had told her he was in a band, and then the next night he said he didn't play an instruments nor did he sing. And when Audrina mentioned the band, he pretended he didn't know what she was talking about. He was also drinking more and more, even arriving drunk to take Audrina out.

"You shouldn't have to be drunk to hang out with me," she told him one night. He only burped in response.

Then the lying got worse. Audrina had seen his type before. Compulsive lying was not cool. There was no way he invented scuba diving, as he had claimed on numerous occasions. Nor was he related to the prince of Monaco. And she knew for a fact that seals and whales were completely different animals. Audrina had gone along with these lies because when she called him on them he got angry, but she was over him at this point, and she needed to let him know.

On the way home from work, she finally decided to dump him. He was supposed to be coming over at 8:30 P.M. He had mentioned something about wanting to play bingo. Audrina didn't know if bingo was some sort of euphemism or if Nick really imagined they were going to a bingo hall.

Audrina got home and was about to step into the shower when her phone rang. She looked at the number and didn't recognize it, but answered it anyway. It was Tony, a friend of Nick's.

"Audrina, it's Tony. I don't know how to tell you this, but Nick's dead."

Audrina dropped the phone in shock. Finally she recovered, bent down, and picked the phone up off the floor.

"Oh my god, what happened?" she asked.

"They're not sure," Tony said. They had found Nick that morning in bed. The funeral was going to be in few days; none of the details had been worked out yet. Audrina hung up the phone and started crying. She felt guilty for wanting to break up with Nick, and she felt incredibly sad that he was dead. Audrina had never before gone out with anyone who wound up dead.

Audrina immediately called Heidi and told her. Heidi couldn't believe it. She hadn't liked Nick, but she didn't think he deserved to die. She offered to come over to Audrina's apartment, but Audrina said she was going to be OK.

Audrina lay awake in bed that night trying to get Nick out of her mind. He lied and drank

and was possessive, but he didn't deserve to die. Eventually, she fell asleep.

The next couple of days went by slowly. Audrina was numb. She went to work but felt like she was just going through the motions. As she was driving home the third day after hearing the terrible news, Audrina realized she hadn't heard back from Tony about the funeral. She didn't have Tony's number in her cell phone, so she decided to call Nick's cell phone, thinking someone from his family might have the phone, and they could tell her about the funeral arrangements.

She called Nick's number. The voice that answered sounded a lot like Nick. Audrina thought it must be his brother or maybe his father. Audrina identified herself and asked who she was speaking to.

"It's me, Nick."

Audrina pulled her car over. Could it really be Nick? She felt like crying. He was alive!

"Nick?" she said in shock.

"Yes."

"I thought . . . I thought you were dead," she said.

"Dead, oh that. That was a joke. My friends thought it—"

Audrina cut him off. "You're an asshole. I really thought you were dead," she yelled, and hung up her phone. She sat in her car, just staring at the traffic, but only for a few minutes. Never one to dwell on the bad things in life or the stupid guys she sometimes got mixed up with, Audrina pulled her car back into the street and headed home.

The Girl Scouts of America Thank You

Lauren and Heidi

The doorbell of the apartment rang early one morning. Heidi had just stepped out of the shower and asked Lauren to get it. Lauren dragged herself out of bed, put on her robe, and walked to the door. She wasn't expecting anybody at such an ungodly hour.

She opened the door, and there stood a young Girl Scout,

probably twelve years old, and a woman, who Lauren presumed was the girl's mother.

"Hi," said the girl. "I've come to deliver your cookies."

"Uh, great," said Lauren, still wiping the sleep from her eyes and trying to comprehend what was going on.

"Twelve boxes of Tagalongs, twelve boxes of Do-si-dos, and twelve boxes of Thin Mints, does that sound right?" the girl wanted to know. The older woman with her remained silent.

Lauren had no idea who had ordered all these cookies. She took the sheet the Girl Scout was handing her. It had Lauren's name on it, so it wasn't like these were the neighbor's cookies and Lauren had gotten them by accident.

The girl and her mother handed Lauren the thirty-six boxes and said good-bye. Lauren said thank you and pushed the door closed. She didn't even know where thirty-six boxes of cookies would fit in the kitchen. Still tired and wanting to go back to sleep, Lauren just walked into her bedroom, put the cookies in the corner on the floor, and climbed back into bed.

A few minutes later, Heidi walked into the living room, grabbed a protein bar from the kitchen, and left for work. Lauren awoke a bit later, showered, and went to work.

Blaine called Lauren into his office and told her she had to run some errands for the magazine. A couple of dresses needed to be taken to a photo shoot in Malibu. Lauren took the dresses to the shoot and then ended up helping out there for a few hours. She got home late that night.

Heidi was working late at Bolthouse, and Jason was out with Jordan, so Lauren decided to go to sleep. The photo shoot had wiped her out.

Due to their work schedules and Lauren's school assignments, Lauren didn't see Heidi until two days later. They were both up and going to work at the same time for once.

Heidi was eating cereal in the living room. When Lauren

walked in, Heidi said, "Did any packages arrive for me yester-day?"

"No," said Lauren, as she poured herself some coffee and sat down on the couch next to Heidi.

"Oh wait, a couple of days ago a Girl Scout brought me thirty-six boxes of cookies," Lauren remembered.

"That's what I'm talking about. Where are they?" Heidi said, very excited.

"In my bedroom," said Lauren.

"Is that where you usually keep your cookies?" Heidi asked sarcastically.

Not waiting for a response, Heidi ran into Lauren's bedroom and yelled happily when she saw the boxes. "They're here! They're here!"

Lauren followed her into the bedroom. "You ordered these?" she asked.

"Yes. The Girl Scouts were in front of the drugstore with their little table, and I couldn't resist," Heidi said.

"Why thirty-six boxes?" Lauren asked.

"I wanted to support the Girl Scouts," said Heidi. "And when I lived at home, we'd get them, but they always ran out way too quick, so I got a lot."

Lauren believed it. It was crazy, but it was Heidi. Lauren had one last question.

"Why did you buy them all with my name?" she said.

"Well, I didn't want anyone thinking I was going to eat thirty-six boxes of cookies," Heidi said, as if the answer was obvious. Lauren supposed it was.

Heidi's Favorite Girl Scout Cookies

1. Thin Mints

2. Do-Si-Dos

3. Tagalongs

4. Samoas

5. All Abouts

South of the Border

Lauren and Jason

Jason had been planning the trip to Mexico for weeks. It was supposed to be a secret from Lauren, but he had mentioned it to so many people at this point that he was sure Lauren must have found out about it somehow. Lauren had a break coming up, but Jason knew that because of work Lauren would have at most five days off in a row. He wanted Lauren to be able to really relax during her vacation, so he had called FIDM to make sure that Lauren didn't have any big tests scheduled the day she would be returning to school.

Heidi knew that Jason was planning a trip to Mexico, but

Jason had intentionally left some of the facts vague. Heidi didn't know the ultimate destination was Cabo San Lucas, or what time of day the flight was. She just knew that Jason was going to surprise Lauren with a trip to Mexico.

"Have you seen my black bikini?" Lauren asked Heidi one day. She had looked all over the apartment, but couldn't find her favorite swimsuit.

"Maybe you left it at your parents' house," Heidi said. Heidi actually knew exactly where the swimsuit was, but she wasn't about to tell Lauren. The black bikini was currently at the bottom of Lauren's pink suitcase, which Heidi and Jason had packed secretly the day before while Lauren was at school. There were also two other bathing suits and a ton of skirts and tops and flip-flops in the suitcase. And if Jason didn't come over soon, Lauren would realize that an awful lot of her clothes were mysteriously missing.

Heidi went into her room and called Jason on her cell phone, but he didn't pick up. She sent him a text message, telling him that Lauren was asking questions about her bikini and if the trip was going to be a surprise, he'd better get over to the apartment soon.

As Heidi was texting Jason, Jason was pulling into the parking lot of the Hillside Villas. Hidden in the trunk of his car was Lauren's suitcase, and Jason's, too. The plane to Cabo was leaving that night and Jason was coming to pick up Lauren for what Lauren thought was going to be a nice dinner at Angeli on Melrose. Instead they would go directly to the airport.

"Are you ready for dinner?" Jason said, as he walked into Lauren and Heidi's apartment.

Heidi made an "it's about time" face at Jason as Lauren walked out of her bedroom, dressed for dinner. Jason kissed Lauren and said they'd better get going if they didn't want to be late.

"Have fun," called Heidi, as Jason and Lauren walked out the door.

Heidi had been acting weird all day, in Lauren's opinion, so when Heidi capped things off by saying, "Have fun," as if Lauren and Jason were off to Disneyland and not just going out to dinner, Lauren decided her roommate was a total nut.

Jason started driving, and soon Lauren realized the car was going south, not west toward the restaurant.

"I thought we were going to Angeli," said Lauren.

"I've got a surprise for you," Jason said.

"A new restaurant?" Lauren said.

"Yeah, in a way," Jason said.

First Heidi was acting weird, now Jason. Something was definitely up.

Jason pulled onto the freeway. Now Lauren was really confused. They never got on the freeway just to go to a restaurant.

"What's going on, Jason?" Lauren demanded.

"What do you mean?" Jason said.

"I mean, where are you taking me?"

"Oh." Jason hesitated. "Well, I thought you might like a few days in Mexico. We're going to the airport."

"Are you serious?" Lauren asked.

Jason assured her that he was, and they drove for a few seconds in silence as Lauren tried to absorb it all. So that was why Heidi had been acting weird. *Mexico!*

"Did you already pack a bag for me?" Lauren asked.

"It's in the trunk," Jason said. "Do you want to go?" he asked.

Of course she did, but she decided to make Jason sweat it out a bit. "Is it Cabo?" she asked, trying to sound as if she were thinking it over.

"Yes."

Lauren waited a few seconds more before she said, "Of course! What time is the flight?"

They made it to the airport with time to spare. Jason had brought Lauren's passport with him, and check-in went smoothly. Once they were on the plane, they shared a passionate kiss. Lauren was overjoyed that Jason had been so thoughtful and wonderful. She couldn't wait to get to Cabo for what she was sure would be an amazing vacation.

Cabo Compromise

Lauren and Jason

Lauren's idea of the perfect vacation was to find a spot on the beach near the hotel early in the morning and not leave until the sun went down. Jason's idea of the perfect vacation was to cram as many activities into the day as possible.

On the flight to Cabo, Jason and Lauren decided to compromise. They would spend half their time on the beach doing nothing, and the other half doing activities: golf, fishing, ATV riding, wake boarding, and sightseeing.

For their first day in Cabo, Jason arranged for the two of them to go fishing in the morning, and then spend time on the beach in the afternoon. Lauren loved fishing. She used to go all the time with her dad and she knew what she was doing out on the water. It was a clear, hot day and the fisherman took them out to a spot he said was good for catching marlin.

Jason didn't have much luck fishing that day, but Lauren did well from the start. After a few nibbles that didn't lead to anything, she felt a small tug on her line and started to reel it in. Jason left his fishing rod to help her. It took a while, but they finally got the fish on board. It was a marlin just over four feet long—the biggest fish Lauren had ever caught! She was so excited, and Jason was excited for her. The rest of the morning in the boat Jason didn't catch anything, but he was still happy for Lauren.

The rest of the day was spent relaxing on the sand, which was one of Lauren's favorite things to do. Lauren told anyone who would listen about the amazingly huge fish she had caught.

The next morning was golf. They played eighteen holes, and Lauren won. Later at the beach she told some new friends a few towels over about how she had caught a huge fish the day before and how she had beat Jason at golf that morning.

The next day Jason said he wanted to go out on the ATV's, but was it OK if he went with a couple of guys he'd met instead of going with Lauren?

"Sure. Have fun. I'll see you at the beach later," Lauren said. More time at the beach was fine with Lauren. If Jason wanted to drive around like a crazy person on the ATV's without her, that was cool with her.

Later that day Jason joined Lauren at the beach. He told her he had flipped his ATV that morning. He was fine—he just had a scraped knee—but he didn't want to go ATVing for a while.

The next morning Jason decided to just hang out at the beach all day with Lauren. It was a vacation, after all, and Jason needed some rest after three days of not catching a fish, losing at golf, and flipping his ATV. And so the rest of their time in Cabo was all about relaxing at the beach.

When they returned to Los Angeles, Lauren felt completely rested and ready to tackle work and school. Jason was glad that Lauren had enjoyed the trip. He had had a fun time, too—even if it hadn't gone exactly as planned.

Lauren's Five Favorite Things About Jason

1. He's not afraid to make fun of me.

2. He'll go shopping with me.

3. He takes care of me when I need it.

4. He's not overly sensitive.

5. He's good at rummy tile.

First-Night Jitters

Jordan and Brian

Tonight was the night. Brian had been dreaming about doing stand-up comedy since he was a kid. He had always admired Jim Carrey, who had gotten his start doing stand-up, and somehow Brian knew, really knew, that stand-up was the right route for him, too.

At their apartment, Brian and Jordan stood in the kitchen going over Brian's act, drinks in their hands.

"I can't believe that after tonight I'll have done stand-up and a dream of mine will have come true," Brian said.

Brian onstage at The Laugh Factory.

They both raised their glasses, said, "Cheers," and took a drink.

Brian was still trying to get his head around the situation. "I was making the guest list for tonight, and I was calling people and saying, 'Yeah, come by. I'm performing at The Laugh Factory.' *The Laugh Factory!* It's world famous."

"I know," Jordan said patiently, having heard all this before.

Brian had used a Sharpie on his arm and written the word *Mom* and a smiley face next to it to give himself strength. Brian's mother had died the previous year, after a long illness, and seeing the word *Mom* on his arm reminded him of his mother's love. Despite his excitement, he knew it was going to be a sentimental night.

Just then his commercial agent called to tell him about an audition the next morning at 9:30.

"Nine-thirty!" said Jordan. "Are you even going to be up at nine-thirty?"

"I will be tomorrow," Brian said with a sigh.

Brian had invited almost fifty people to come see him, including his agent from Paradigm. William Morris was sending some agents, too. A lot of VIPs were going to see Brian tonight, and the importance of the evening was beginning to sink in.

"I could throw up right now," he said to Jordan.

"Just not on me, please," Jordan replied.

Brian paced in the small kitchen, telling Jordan bits of his stand-up routine. He had been practicing all day, running through different combinations of words until he found just the right delivery.

"Is this any good?" he asked, suddenly nervous.

"Dude, it's hilarious," Jordan assured him.

"I've been practicing all day. I feel like I've really been practicing my whole life, you know?" Brian said. "I feel like I'll always remember this day. The first time I ever did stand-up."

Jordan knew that Brian was beginning to hype himself up, so he just let him do it.

"I don't know why I've been scared for so long. I feel good," Brian said.

"Good and exhausted," Jordan added. Jordan could see the effects on Brian of staying up late and continuously going over his material.

Finally, it was time to leave. On their way out the door, Brian said, "It's only three minutes, but it could be the start of something huge." He closed the door behind them and headed out for The Laugh Factory.

Brian's Favorite Comedians/Actors

1. Jim Carrey
2. Jerry Seinfeld
3. Dane Cook
4. Johnny Depp
5. Kevin James
6. Chris Rock
7. Dave Chapelle
8. Vince Vaughn
9. Ben Stiller
10. Owen Wilson

Bringing Down the House

Brian and Jordan

Brian and Jordan parked the car behind The Laugh Factory and walked to the front of the club. Other comedians and guests were milling around outside. Open Mic Night drew an eclectic mix of people. Some of the comedians were first-timers like Brian, but there were other more seasoned performers who had a different vibe. They were a little more self-assured and didn't have the same manic energy that the first-timers were exhibiting.

Brian was naturally drawn to the veterans and struck up a conversation with one of them. It was then that he got some news that hit him like a ton of bricks.

"They don't allow any swearing in your act. It all has to be G-rated," the comedian said.

Brian suddenly felt like he was out of breath. He walked over to where Jordan was standing and whispered, "I don't know what I'm going to do." He explained his dilemma.

"You're gonna be fine," Jordan said. But privately, Jordan wasn't so sure it would all work out. A lot of Brian's funniest material was laced with swear words. Brian would figure a way around it; he had to. Just then Brian's friends and guests started arriving, including Heidi and Audrina, Lauren and Jason, and even Whitney. There was a large crowd of people outside the club as the doors were opened and performers and audience members walked into the club together.

Brian was nervous, but kept it under control. The night's comedians were cordoned off to the side of the stage where the MC went over the rules. The first thing he mentioned was the no-swearing rule. He then pointed to the red light that would signal the comedians when they had ten seconds left in their act. As the MC talked, Brian figured out a way to still do his act without the swearing. He could imply the offending words by leading up to them, but not actually saying them. Like "What the . . ." and then instead of following through, he could make a face that would suggest the word without offending anybody. The rest of the rules were just a blur. Brian knew what he needed to know. Three minutes. No swearing. Red light.

Brian began focusing on hyping himself up with a positive interior monologue. He told himself, *I'm a superstar, and all these people are going to find that out tonight. I've been thinking about this my whole life. I own this place. It's time to show these people I am the best. It's showtime.*

When his name was announced, he walked up onstage, the energy coursing through him. He grabbed the mic and literally jumped up and down with excitement.

In the audience Jordan was holding his breath. Brian launched into his routine, and people started laughing. Not just the people Brain had invited, but everyone. Even the other comedians were laughing. Jordan knew that other comedians could be the toughest audience, and Brian was winning them over. He was in the zone. All the hours of practicing in front of the mirror were finally paying off. And then Brian saw the red light. He couldn't believe it. It was over. It felt like he had been onstage thirty seconds. Brian wrapped it up, thanked the audience, and said good night.

The audience erupted in a huge round of applause. Brian looked down at the *Mom* and the smiley face he had written on his arm. He knew his mother would be proud of him. It was a good feeling. The greatest.

That's *Ms.* Fix-It to You

Whitney

There were certain days that Whitney worked alone at *Teen Vogue*, because Lauren was at school, and today was one of those days. Whitney missed the easy camaraderie she shared with Lauren, but there was still work to be done. She was in the middle of doing some research for Lisa Love when Blaine walked in.

"We're going to be shooting 'A Room of My Own' tomorrow, and I'd like you to assist the stylist," he said. "She'll be calling you in a little while to tell you everything you'll need to know."

"A Room of My Own" was a feature on the last page of every issue of the magazine. The article consisted of a full-page photograph of a young girl standing in her room, accompanied by text about who the girl is and how she made her room look a certain way. It had always been one of Whitney's favorite features.

"Wow, that sounds terrific," said Whitney, trying to hide her excitement.

The stylist called later in the afternoon and told Whitney everything she would need for the photo shoot. Whitney couldn't wait for the shoot to begin.

Whitney was up early the next morning and left the house quickly; there was no way she was going to be late, not today. She arrived at the office early and started packing up the clothes needed for the shoot. Sometimes the girls featured wore their own clothes, and sometimes they wore a couple of pieces the magazine supplied. Whitney got the clothes steamer ready and collapsed a couple of clothing racks. By the time Blaine came into the office, Whitney was ready to leave for the shoot. Blaine was impressed with Whitney being so on top of everything, and told her so. They both carried everything down to the car and loaded it up with their gear. Since Whitney had loaded and unloaded all the bags, steamer, and racks before, she had worked out a system to get all the stuff in and out of the car quickly and economically. It was a lot of manual labor, but Whitney just looked at it like an extra workout. Blaine, again, was impressed with how quickly Whitney got everything done.

The shoot was at a house in the San Fernando Valley. Whitney had made a map from Mapquest to make sure they didn't get lost, and sure enough, they didn't. After unloading the car, Whitney met the stylist for the shoot, a woman named Meg, who showed her where to set up the clothing racks and the steamer. Meg then introduced Whitney to the high school girl whose room they were shooting, as well as the girl's parents.

Upstairs, the girl's bedroom was painted a gorgeous periwinkle blue with a subtle soft yellow border; Whitney loved it and complimented the girl on her color choice. Whitney had a lot of clothes to steam, though, so she returned downstairs to get started. That was when she made a terrible discovery: The steamer wasn't working. She thought perhaps the outlet she was using wasn't working, so she tried another one in the hallway. Still no luck. She didn't know what to do. She didn't want to ask Blaine or Meg about it, but she had to figure out some way to get the wrinkles out of the clothes. She thought about asking the people who owned the house if they had an iron and ironing board she could use, but she wasn't sure that was the right way to go, either.

Finally, she decided to inspect the steamer itself. Maybe there was something obviously broken, and she could just fix it. She had never been accused of being the fix-it type at home, but she knew she had to do *something*.

She got down on her hands and knees, and took a look at the steamer. It was a simple machine with just an on-and-off switch and a plastic ball that held the water for steaming. As Whitney looked closer, she saw the problem. The electrical cord had frayed right where it attached to the steamer. All she needed to fix it was some electrical tape.

Whitney went into the kitchen and asked the girl's mother if she had any electrical tape that Whitney could use. The woman directed Whitney to a worktable in the garage, where Whitney might be able to find what she needed. Luckily for Whitney, the roll of tape was right where the woman said it would be.

Back at the steamer, Whitney carefully wrapped the cord with electrical tape and made sure there were no loose wires. She plugged in the steamer and, lo and behold, it worked!

The rest of the day went off without a hitch. Meg, Blaine, and the photographer got everything they needed. Whitney put the electrical tape back in the garage and made a mental note to mention the broken steamer to Blaine the next day so that it could be repaired or replaced.

The next day at work Whitney walked into Blaine's office to let him know about the steamer.

"I was about to come find you," Blaine said. "I just got off the phone with Meg. She was very impressed with your work yesterday. She called to ask if she could use you to assist her on a photo shoot for another magazine."

Whitney couldn't believe it. "Wow. Am I allowed to work on a shoot for another magazine?" she asked.

"You are, if it doesn't interfere with your schedule with us," Blaine told her. "Oh, and nice fix on the steamer."

Whitney was completely surprised. "How did you know about it?" she asked.

"The girl's mother at the house told me before we left yesterday. Way to save the day, Whitney," Blaine said.

It was just a frayed cord and a piece of tape, but Whitney walked back to her desk feeling like a superstar.

Happiness Is a Bacon Chili Cheese Dog

Jordan and Brian

"It was dream come true," Brian said. He and Jordan were driving to Pink's hot dog stand, a Los Angeles institution. It had been in the same spot since 1939 and boasted every kind of hot dog imaginable.

Jordan pulled the car into the parking lot. Brian was still high from his stand-up performance the previous evening. They got out of the car and got in line.

"You killed 'em last night. Killed 'em," Jordan said.

"Are we all going to Koi tonight?" Brian asked.

"It's on. You, me, and Heidi celebrating how well you did last night. You know, the food there is a bit different than here," Jordan cracked.

"I know. That's why I love living here. You can eat at a hot dog stand for lunch and then have some of the best sushi on the planet for dinner," Brian said.

"It is pretty sweet," agreed Jordan.

Finally, it was their turn to order.

"I'll have a New York Dog with sauerkraut," said Brian. Jordan went with the Bacon Chili Cheese Dog.

"It was hard to focus last night after I got offstage," Brian said. "Like the time onstage went so, so fast, and then I don't remember much of the rest of the night."

"The booze might have something to do with that," Jordan said.

"You never know," Brian said with a grin.

They picked up their hot dogs and found some seats. On the walls were hundreds of framed head shots of celebrities who had eaten at Pink's.

"Someday, Brian, someday," said Jordan, referring to the photographs.

"Me, Ryan Seacrest, and Martha Stewart. That's quite some company to have," joked Brian.

The guys devoured their hot dogs and washed them down with grape soda.

"It was really great that so many people came out to see me last night," Brian said.

"You've got a lot of friends," Jordan said.

"I just wanted to say thank you for all your support over the last couple of weeks; it really meant a lot to me," Brian said.

"Shut up and eat your hot dog. But you're welcome," Jordan said.

All in all, it was another good day in Los Angeles. Brian was looking forward to going to Koi that night, but right then he decided to start a new tradition. Every time he performed in Los Angeles, Brian would go to Pink's the next day for lunch. It was a great way to start off the day.

Jordan's Favorite Hot Dogs at Pink's

1. Bacon Chili Cheese Dog

2. Double Bacon Chili Cheese Dog

3. Guadalajara Dog

4. Coleslaw Dog

5. The Martha Stewart Dog

Water Sports

Lauren, Heidi, Jason, and Jordan

Jason and Jordan had wanted to go Jet Skiing for ages, but just hadn't been able to find the time. Finally, on a nasty sweltering day, they decided to head down to Marina Del Rey and rent some Jet Skis. Both guys had ridden Jet Skis before, so they didn't have to take lessons and figure out how to maneuver the things. It was just a day in the sun in Southern California, taking it easy. When they got back home that evening, it was all they could talk about.

"The water was unbelievable," said Jason, as he walked into the apartment and kissed Lauren hello.

"So you guys had a good day?" she asked.

"It was tremendous," said Jordan. "The best day in a long time."

Heidi came out of her bedroom and planted a big kiss on Jordan's mouth.

"I wanna go," she said.

"We were just talking about that on the way back here," Jason said.

"Yeah. You guys aren't working tomorrow," Jordan said.

"And no school," Jason added.

"We're all going Jet Skiing. We're all going Jet Skiing," Heidi said with a singsong voice.

"I can't wait," Lauren said.

The next morning was sunny and bright. Perfect weather for being on the water. Everyone got up early and packed a bag with extra clothes and swimsuits and flip-flops. The four of them piled into Jason's car and headed to Marina Del Rey.

Unfortunately, once they hit Santa Monica, the sun disappeared.

"It's looking cloudy out," said Heidi.

"It'll be sunny down by the water," Jordan replied confidently.

Nothing was going to stop the four of them from ripping it up on the water. But as they got closer, the weather wasn't clearing up; if anything, it was getting cloudier and the temperature was noticeably cooler.

"Was it this overcast yesterday?" Lauren asked as Jason parked the car.

"Pretty much," Jason said. *Great.*

Everyone got out of the car and could feel the cold wind coming off the ocean as they headed to the rental shop, which

faced the marina and was packed floor to ceiling with every kind of Jet Ski on the market.

At the rental counter, Heidi whispered to Lauren, "I'm freezing."

"So am I," Lauren said.

Down on the dock, they picked out their Jet Skis.

"I want the yellow one," Heidi declared, sitting down on it to stake her claim. Lauren went with a blue-and-white model, while Jordan and Jason each got red. All four started up their Jet Skis, and with the sound of splashing water in their wake, headed out into the ocean.

The first thing Lauren noticed was that the water was freezing.

"It'll warm up once we're out here for a bit," Jason said as he rode beside her.

Jason and Jordan seemed to be the only ones having fun, racing each other and making huge arching splashes.

Lauren couldn't believe how cold it was. No matter what Jason said, with no sun out, it didn't seem likely that the air or the water was going to get any warmer.

"Are we at the North Pole?" Heidi shouted to Lauren through chattering teeth. "My arms are seriously frozen," she said.

"Whose idea was this?" Lauren wanted to know.

The boys had had enough of splashing each other and were now setting their sights on Lauren and Heidi. The chase was on, and it didn't take long for Jordan and Jason to overtake them.

"It's already freezing out here. You better not splash me, Jordan Patrick Eubanks," Heidi yelled. But it was too late; a wide wall of cold water came down on her and her Jet Ski. Heidi was not happy.

Lauren was still maneuvering in the hope that Jason wouldn't splash her when, without any notice, her Jet Ski konked out and she wasn't moving, only drifting. Jason immediately motored over to see if she was all right.

"I'm fine. It's the Jet Ski that's dead," she said.

Jason asked her to try to start it up again, but it was no use. Jason told her he would go back to the dock and get the rental people to come out and take a look at it. He raced over to the dock and came back with the rental guys on a small motorboat. Lauren hopped up onto the boat.

"They say you can come in and get another Jet Ski that works back at the dock," Jason said.

"I'm freezing. I don't want to go back out," Lauren said.

"Seriously? Aren't you having fun?"

"I'm having fun being with you, but I don't want to freeze anymore," she said.

Jason hugged her tight and told her he was going to call it a day. They needed to get back to Los Angeles where they knew the sun was shining. He waved in Jordan and Heidi.

In the car on the way back to the apartment, Heidi summed up the day. "That was like the trip from hell. I think my ass is frozen." Lauren, Jason, and Jordan all laughed and agreed they wouldn't go Jet Skiing again until it really, really warmed up.

Ladies Who Lunch

Lauren, Heidi, and Audrina

Lauren, Heidi, and Audrina hadn't all been to lunch together in forever, so Lauren suggested it to Heidi one night at the apartment.

"That's a fantastic idea," said Heidi, a little too quickly. "I'll call Audrina and tell her to come. How's Wednesday?"

Lauren knew work had been bugging Heidi, but judging from Heidi's overjoyed speed in her reaction to lunch, Lauren could tell work must have really been bumming Heidi out. But Lauren knew from experience that if Heidi wanted to talk about something, she would in her own time, so Lauren gave her roommate some space.

"I love Wednesday," Lauren assured her, as Heidi dialed the phone.

Luckily, Wednesday turned out to be a beautiful day, and the three girls met up at the Quality Café. It was roughly equidistant from all three girls' offices, and you could eat outside—a definite plus on such a beautiful day.

Audrina was the last to arrive. "I went to this Brazilian dance class. You dance spinning around. It was so hard; my legs are killing me," she said as she sat down.

"Hi, Audrina," Heidi said pointedly.

"Sorry, hi," said Audrina.

The waiter arrived to take their order. Heidi ordered the seafood salad, Audrina got a chicken Caesar salad, and Lauren opted for the avocado mushroom omelet.

After the waiter left, Heidi wasted no time in turning the

conversation to her situation at work. "I am so ready to quit," she said.

"Every day she comes home and says she's quitting," Lauren told Audrina.

"It's just so boring. I mean it. I want to quit," complained Heidi.

Audrina was trying to think of something positive to say. She knew Heidi liked the nightlife aspect of working at Bolthouse Productions.

"You like working at LAX, don't you?" Audrina prodded.

"I guess so," admitted Heidi, "but I hate it when Jordan comes by, because I can't be with him, and I have to watch other girls hit on him."

Lauren had heard most of this before, but nonetheless listened as Heidi listed everything she disliked about working. Then Audrina pointed out, "If you want to be independent, you have to work, and it's not always going to be fun." Lauren agreed; in her opinion, Heidi needed to grow up a little.

Heidi absorbed what Audrina said and for a moment, at least, came to realize that working was a part of her life right now.

Lunch arrived quickly, and the girls began eating.

As they finished up their meal Heidi said what the other girls had only been thinking. "I don't want to go back to work."

"Neither do I," Audrina said.

"And neither do I," Lauren echoed.

Unfortunately, they didn't have any choice in the matter, so the three girls regretfully parted and headed back to their offices, wishing the weekend would arrive just a little bit sooner.

L.A. Life

Lauren: Loves having her own apartment in L.A. She orders in takeout almost every night, and she can be as messy as she wants.

Whitney: Los Angeles is the best of both worlds, the perfect mix of the beach and city life.

Audrina: In L.A., everyone talks about themselves because they're all aspiring actors and musicians.

Heidi: Spotting celebrities everywhere has become a hobby. It's like a zoo.

Meet the Conrads

Lauren and Heidi

"A re we meeting them there, or are they coming here?" Heidi wanted to know. She was in her bedroom, yelling across the living room to Lauren's room. Jim and Kathy, Lauren's parents, were in Los Angeles to pick up their new car, and had offered to take Lauren and Heidi to dinner.

"We're meeting them there," Lauren replied. She was still trying to figure out which top to wear.

"Go with the black one," Heidi advised, as she walked into Lauren's room. Heidi was already dressed in skinny jeans and a light brown top.

"Is Jason coming tonight?" Heidi asked. Heidi wasn't sure how things stood at the moment with Jason and Lauren's dad. Jason and Jim hadn't always seen eye-to-eye on everything in the past, but that was a long time ago, and as far as Heidi knew they got along well now.

"No, he has other dinner plans tonight," Lauren replied.

Lauren took Heidi's advice and went with the black top. Soon enough they were out the door and on their way to Campanile for dinner.

The girls walked into the restaurant to find Jim and Kathy already seated. There were hugs and kisses all around. Heidi hadn't seen Lauren's parents in two months and was happy to be at dinner with them.

Looking over the menus, Heidi told everyone that when she was younger she used to order based on price.

"You ordered the most expensive thing?" asked Lauren.

"Of course," said Heidi.

Lauren then told her parents the story of the Jet Skis. Jim couldn't believe they went on Jet Skis without wet suits or booties or gloves.

"Why'd you go?" he asked.

"Because the boys wanted to," Lauren explained.

"I hope that wasn't the only reason," Jim said.

"No, we wanted to go, too," Lauren assured her father.

"How long has it been now, with you and Jason?" Jim asked.

"I don't know when our anniversary is," Lauren said. "We don't have a date for when we officially started going out."

"How about the night of the fashion show in Laguna Beach," Kathy said snidely.

Lauren looked at her mother, shocked and hurt, as Heidi gaped beside her. The fashion show had been the night Jason cheated on Lauren with his old girlfriend, Jessica. Why was

Kathy bringing that up now? "That's a mean thing to say," Lauren said, her eyes stinging.

"I know. I'm sorry, honey," Kathy said, regret in her voice.

After that, all four of them did their best to put the emotional upset behind them and revive the pleasant mood they had been enjoying at the beginning of dinner. Lauren found herself more grateful than ever that Heidi had come along—her roommate always managed to keep a conversation moving. As if on cue, Heidi started talking about Jordan, going on and on about his latest adventures, and Lauren breathed a sigh of relief.

"What does Jordan want to do?" Kathy asked.

"He wants to record an album, and then he wants to get into real estate," Heidi said.

"Maybe he could be real estate partners with Jason," Jim said.

"They're already partners in everything. They work out together; they get their hair cut together," Heidi said.

Jim raised an eyebrow at that.

"Dad," Lauren said warningly.

After they finished eating, it was time to say good-bye. Heidi thanked Jim and Kathy for the dinner. Lauren hugged her mom and dad good night. The evening could have gone better, but all in all Lauren counted herself lucky to have such great parents.

East Coast, West Coast

Lauren, Whitney, and Heidi

Sometimes, when you can forget about work and school, you can imagine your life is a string of lovely dinner dates. Shortly after their dinner with the Conrads, Lauren and Heidi were out again, this time to celebrate unexpectedly walking the runway in the DKNY Jeans fashion show. They had also invited Whitney and a girl named Juliana, a *Teen Vogue* intern from the New York office, to join them. Juliana had come out to assist on the fashion show and had to fly back the following day.

Whitney was happy to be out at dinner with her friends, but what she really wanted was to hear about what Juliana did in New York. The idea of being a *Teen Vogue* intern in New York seemed extra glamorous to Whitney.

"To Whitney," the girls said in unison, raising their glasses.

"How did it feel?" Heidi asked.

"I don't remember," Whitney admitted. She remembered walking up the stairs to get to the runway, and she remembered coming off the runway, but she didn't remember her time out under the lights.

Then Heidi noticed that there was lobster on the menu. "I love lobster. It's my favorite food. I could eat twenty lobsters a day. I'm obsessed with it," she said in her excitable way.

Juliana thought Heidi was hilarious.

The waiter came over and the girls ordered their food. Heidi couldn't believe that Whitney and Lauren had worked so hard all week for just ten minutes on the runway. Juliana said that in

New York, they would have up to three fashion shows on the same day.

"There'd be a lot of screaming and yelling, and then ten minutes of chaos," said Juliana.

The girls wanted to hear more, so Juliana filled them in on the life of a New York intern.

"They're usually really long days. We start early and go home most days at eight at night," said Juliana.

"Oh my god. Do you have a social life?" said Whitney, and then caught herself. "I don't mean that in a mean way."

"You end up hanging out with the people from work," Juliana said with a shrug.

The girls were intrigued, listening to Juliana's New York experience.

"In the New York office, if you make one little mess up, you're fired," said Juliana.

"That's not fair," said Whitney. "You're supposed to make mistakes while you're learning."

"There are just so many people in New York who would kill for an internship at the magazine that they just take the next person," Juliana said matter-of-factly.

"But nobody's perfect," Whitney pointed out.

"You'd do great there, Lauren," Heidi said sarcastically.

Lauren glared at her.

Whitney leaned over and asked Juliana in a whisper, "You like it here, though, don't you?"

"I love it. It's really exciting. Each day is different. You never know what you're going to do," said Juliana.

The evening ended, and the girls all headed home. The talk with Juliana had given Whitney a lot to think about. New York sounded kind of scary, and Whitney wasn't sure if she really wanted to make working there a goal. As she drove home she consoled herself that she had plenty of time to think about the future.

Cupcake for Two

Audrina

Audrina only got an hour for lunch, so she liked to go places that were close to work. She had never been to M Café, but it was just a couple of blocks away from Quixote Studios, and she had heard people at work talking about how good it was. It was a health food place, and Audrina was always trying to eat healthy, so she thought she'd give it a try.

Audrina liked the M Café from the moment she walked in. The only thing she didn't like was the line. Every minute in line was a minute she couldn't be sitting down, enjoying her food before it was time to head back to work. The line looked so long that Audrina thought about going to one of her usual spots down the street instead, where she could pop in and out in fifteen minutes, and still have some time to walk around and shop.

As she was waiting in line, contemplating whether to leave, a guy stepped into line behind her. Audrina caught a glimpse of him and thought he looked cute, so she decided to wait it out.

Audrina turned her head, pretending to look around the café as she strained to get a better look at the guy behind her.

He had dark brown hair and deep dark eyes. Audrina turned back around. While Audrina had been trying to check him out nonchalantly, this guy had been staring at her. His eyes never left her face.

He looked liked he was in a band. If Audrina had a type of guy she liked, and she hated even admitting that she had a type, it would be guys in bands.

The line started moving, and Audrina scanned the posted menu. Even though it was a health food place it looked like there were plenty of yummy things to eat. In a bakery display case to the right of the counter were all sorts of delicious-looking cookies and cakes. Audrina spotted a single chocolate cupcake on the middle rack in the case and decided that was going to be hers. She'd order a salad and the cupcake. Maybe it wasn't the healthiest lunch in the world, but at that moment Audrina thought it sounded perfect.

As the line moved forward, Audrina glanced back again at the guy. This time he smiled at her. She smiled back.

The line moved and now there was only one person in front of her. She looked over to the case to make sure the lone chocolate cupcake was still there. It was.

"Are you thinking about that cupcake?" the guy said from behind her.

"What?" Audrina stammered, surprised that cute-band-guy had actually spoken to her.

"I saw you looking at the last cupcake, and I was wondering if you're going to order it," he said.

"I was thinking about it," Audrina admitted.

"That's your right. I mean, it looks delicious, but I want it," he said.

Audrina almost said, "Too bad," but instead said, "You can have it if you want. If taking away my cupcake makes you happy, then you can do it."

He smiled.

"Chocolate is my favorite," he said apologetically.

"Chocolate is my favorite, too."

When it was Audrina's turn to order, she asked for the salad and an Arnold Palmer to drink. No cupcake.

The cute guy behind her spoke again. "We could share it. You have half, and I have half."

"That might work," Audrina said.

Audrina paid for her lunch, and the guy paid for the cupcake at his insistence. The two of them found a small table in the corner of the restaurant and sat down with their backs to the windows.

Audrina realized she was having lunch with a cute band guy and she didn't even know his name.

"My name is Audrina," she volunteered.

"My name's Shannon," he said.

They looked at each other and smiled. Then Shannon began cutting the cupcake in half.

"I probably wouldn't have eaten the whole thing anyway," Audrina said.

Shannon and Audrina ended up talking easily for her whole lunch break. Sure enough, Shannon was in a band, just as Audrina suspected. Audrina felt as if she and Shannon had known each other a long time.

After all the talking and eating had ended, Audrina had to race back to the office to get there on time, but not before Shannon asked for Audrina's phone number. She couldn't wait for him to call.

Frozen Yogurt for Everyone

Lauren and Jason

Lauren had arrived at *Teen Vogue* early Wednesday morning for a full day in the intern closet. Whitney was at school that day, so Lauren would be on her own.

The first order of business was loading up all the clothes used for the most recent cover shoot. The garments had to be packed up and shipped back to the design houses that had sent them. The designers were very particular about how their clothes were handled. The clothes needed to be returned just as *Teen Vogue* had received them, which meant Lauren had to pay precise attention to her packing. Dresses needed to be folded perfectly.

Lauren remembered one time in particular when she and Whitney were new at *Teen Vogue* and had packed one designer's clothes in the wrong type of box. Blaine had pointed out their mistake just before the FedEx guy arrived to pick up the package. The girls had to make a mad scramble to get the clothes repacked in time. Thankfully, Lisa Love had never found out about that near snafu.

Lauren was preparing all the boxes and bags for packing when her phone rang.

"Hi," Jason said, when Lauren answered. "How many people are there in your office today?"

"I don't know. Whitney's gone, so about ten people including me. Why do you want to know?" Lauren said.

"I was just trying to figure something out. See you later."

Lauren had no idea what her boyfriend was up to, but she had no time to worry about it. Blaine had just piled some clothes on Lauren's desk and told her they needed to be steamed for a shoot the next day. It was the worst day for Whitney not to be there.

Besides the clothes packing and steaming, Lauren also had to go on the morning coffee run. Luckily only three people wanted something from The Coffee Bean & Tea Leaf that morning, so Lauren had no problem bringing the coffee back up to the office.

The day dragged on, filled with steaming and packing. Then Blaine told her he needed some belt and scarf research done for a shoot the following week. Lauren was so busy she missed lunch and by four P.M. she was ready to lie down and take a nap, but there was still a lot of work to do.

Suddenly, Jason entered the intern closet. He was holding a bag from a trendy frozen yogurt shop.

"No you didn't!" was Lauren's first reaction. She gave Jason a huge hug. From inside the bag he pulled out a cup of frozen yogurt. It was still cold and unmelted.

"How did you manage to keep it cold?" Lauren wanted to know.

The store was twenty minutes away in West Hollywood. On every day of the week, every moment that the store was open, there was a line out the door that was at least a thirty-minute wait. It was quite a time commitment to get this particular frozen yogurt.

"The car has a built-in fridge," said Jason casually.

Lauren took a bite. "Oh my god, it's so good. This is just what I needed," she said blissfully.

Jason opened the bag and Lauren could see that Jason had bought enough for everyone in the office. Lauren knew that Blaine and Lisa Love both loved the frozen delight, and couldn't wait to surprise them with the unexpected treat.

Lauren and Jason left the intern closet and went to Blaine's office first. He was on the phone, but when Lauren handed him the icy-cold frozen yogurt he hung up immediately.

"Thank you. This is just what I needed. And not even melted! Thank you," Blaine gushed.

Lauren asked if it would be okay to knock on Lisa Love's door. Blaine said it would be fine, and then went back to eating.

Lisa Love was at her desk looking over some photos for the upcoming issue. When she looked up and saw Lauren and Jason, she smiled.

"I've got a frozen yogurt here for you if you'd like it," Lauren said.

"Lauren, you know I love it! Thank you so much," Lisa said.

Lauren and Jason then handed out the rest of the frozen yogurt to the other editors and assistants. It felt like Christmas. No one turned down a gift of free frozen yogurt.

Lauren and Jason went back into the closet and ate their delicious treat. After they were done, Jason helped Lauren pack the rest of the clothes. It had turned into a wonderful day, all because of Jason and some frozen yogurt.

You Really Can Find Anything on Craigslist

Jordan

It was getting close to Christmas and Jordan wasn't sure what he was going to get Heidi. He lay in bed, while Heidi puttered around the kitchen getting her breakfast before she had to go to work, and tried to figure it out. They had talked about a dog, but nothing had been completely decided, and he didn't know if that was the right way to go.

Heidi came back into the bedroom with a bowl of cereal in hand and sat down on the bed next to Jordan. She turned on the TV and ran through the channels until she found *SpongeBob SquarePants,* her favorite show to watch before work. As she sat and ate, a commercial came on for a new DVD collection of *The Ren & Stimpy Show.*

"I used to love that show," said Jordan.

"Me too," said Heidi, and she gave Jordan a kiss, like it was a prize for having the same taste in cartoons.

"Which one was the dog?" she asked.

"Ren was the dog, and Stimpy was the cat," said Jordan.

"What kind of dog?" Heidi playfully demanded.

"I think he's a Chihuahua," Jordan said, proving himself to be a true aficionado.

"That's the kind of dog I want, a tiny little Chihuahua," Heidi pronounced. Then she looked at the clock. "Oh, I gotta get to work." She kissed Jordan

Jordan and Heidi goofing around during the holidays.

again, took another spoonful of cereal, and left.

Jordan instantly went online and started looking up Chihuahuas. After reading a few pages about the dogs, he decided that a Chihuahua would indeed be the perfect Christmas present.

Jordan did some searching and found a guy on Craigslist. com who was selling teacup Chihuahuas, the tiniest breed of Chihuahuas. The only problem was the guy lived in Fresno, California, which was way too far to drive for a dog. Jordan e-mailed the guy to see if they could work something out. It turned out the guy, whose name was Steve, was coming down to Los

Angeles in a day or so with a dog for someone else. If Steve and Jordan could come to some sort of an arrangement, then Steve would bring down a dog for Jordan, too. They agreed on a price and a delivery date. Jordan was happy and relieved that he had figured out what to get Heidi for Christmas.

When Steve, the dog guy, arrived in Los Angeles, he called Jordan to set up a meeting place. Jordan got the call while he was shopping at Tower Records on Sunset Boulevard. Jordan asked if Steve knew where Tower Records was. Steve said he could be there in fifteen minutes.

Fifteen minutes later, Jordan was in the parking lot holding a tiny Chihuahua puppy. Jordan handed Steve the money, they shook hands, and that was it. Jordan had bought his first Christmas present for Heidi.

At Jordan and Brian's apartment, the dog acclimated herself

Cute and cuddly Bella.

as soon as Jordan put her down on the rug. Jordan couldn't believe that such a little dog could urinate for so long.

That night Brian came home to an apartment that reeked of urine. Then Jordan broke the news. The dog was going to have to stay at their apartment for three days until Christmas. Brian understood, but he made a deal with Jordan that Jordan would have to clean up after the dog—and try to keep it from peeing on the floor.

Life Behind the Velvet Rope

Heidi

"It's really hard for me to sit behind a desk; I'm just not that person," Heidi said in a whisper. "I am so bored I might have to shoot myself."

She was talking to her coworker Elodie, who was sitting twenty feet away in the office.

"Heidi, every day can't be great. Tonight is LAX; we'll have fun there," Elodie responded. She had heard Heidi's rant about not liking the office and being bored about a hundred times, and that was just in the last two days.

Heidi didn't want to quit, but she didn't want to be in the office so much, either. She loved working the clubs, but she wanted

more. Heidi had spoken to her boss, Brent, about it and he had told her to be patient, that as soon as other nights opened up, she could work those, too.

Work seemed to be taking forever to end, but finally six P.M. rolled around. Heidi raced home and had dinner, then got ready for LAX. She put on a black top, a black skirt, and her favorite red Moschino shoes, and she was ready for work, the kind of work that she actually liked.

Heidi's job at the door was to greet guests and make sure that the people who had made reservations for table service were being looked after. Table service was one way into the club. You could call earlier in the week and reserve a table and say how many people you were bringing. Depending on how many people you had with you, table service could get really expensive really quickly, but the kind of people who got table service usually didn't care about that. They just wanted to get into the club. Another way in was to wait in line, and the line moved really slowly. A third way in was, of course, to be a celebrity—celebrities never had to wait. Heidi's job was to greet the table service customers, greet the celebrities, and tell everyone else to wait in line.

The night was going well, with the club full and a long line of people waiting to get in. Suddenly, a guy who had been waiting approached Heidi. She thought he looked kind of cute and was considering letting him inside, but then the guy looked down at

Heidi's red shoes and said, "Click your heels three times, Doro-thy, and end up in my bed."

Heidi was shocked. She'd thought the guy might compliment her, not offer such a crude invitation. What a jerk.

"You're disgusting," she told him. She called over one of the doormen and told him to never let that lame-o in the club. The guy slinked away as Heidi glared after him.

Later that night Heidi told Elodie what the guy had said.

"Before he said anything I thought he was kinda cute, and I was going let him in the club. But then he opened his mouth," Heidi said.

"They can't all be winners," Elodie said wisely.

No, they can't, thought Heidi. It had been a bad day and a bad evening. The only thing Heidi had to look forward to was Privilege on Friday night.

Speak the Words on Your Lips

Lauren

It was another day in the *Teen Vogue* intern closet for Whitney and Lauren. Whitney was telling Lauren about all the fun she had with her boyfriend, David, over the weekend, when in walked Blaine and Kimball. Kimball was another editor at *Teen Vogue*. Although the girls knew who Kimball was, they had never met him directly before today.

Kimball told them that he was going to be interviewing Natasha Bedingfield on Wednesday, and he wanted both girls to be there to help him.

"I have school on Wednesday," said Whitney.

"I don't," said Lauren happily. Whitney looked over at Lauren and could see that Lauren was just teasing her.

"I met Natasha at New York Fashion Week and fell in love with her," Kimball explained. "She's just moved from England to L.A. to record her second album, and she asked me to come by the studio."

Lauren was extremely excited to meet Natasha Bedingfield. She was a big fan—she even had Natasha's hit song "Unwritten" as the ringtone on her cell phone.

"So, Lauren," Kimball said, interrupting her reverie, "you're going to go with me, and I'll need you to do research on L.A. designers. Natasha is from England, and I'm not sure how many L.A. designers she knows, so we'll be introducing some to her."

Blaine suggested Lauren write up some sample questions for Natasha that Kimball might be able to use in the interview.

Kimball and Blaine said their good-byes and left. Lauren hadn't written a lot before, so she asked Whitney if they could go over the questions together. Whitney said she would help, even though she was jealous she'd have to miss out on meeting the pop star.

"She's from London, right?" Lauren said.

"Why not ask, like, what are her favorite stores in London?" Whitney suggested.

"That's a good idea," Lauren said.

"Thanks. What about the *Teen Vogue* favorite?" Whitney asked.

"How would you describe your personal style?" both girls said simultaneously and then cracked up laughing. That question seemed to be used in every interview that *Teen Vogue* published.

"How about, 'Who's your fashion icon?' " Whitney said.

"I hate that question," said Lauren, but wrote it down anyway. "I guess because I don't have a fashion icon, I always think it's a bit of an odd question. There's no one person whose wardrobe I would love completely."

"I know what you mean. I like people who try new things," Whitney said.

"Me too," said Lauren.

Wednesday arrived quickly. Kimball came over to Lauren's desk and told her he was impressed with her questions for Natasha. Then Kimball asked if Lauren would like to conduct part of the interview herself.

"You mean, actually ask Natasha Bedingfield questions?" asked Lauren.

"Yes, that's what I mean," replied Kimball.

THE HILLS

"I would love to." Lauren couldn't believe her luck.

Lauren and Kimball took a car to the studio in the Hollywood hills at Natasha's record producer's house. It was an intimate setting surrounded by trees.

Kimball still planned to show Natasha the works of some L.A. designers, in addition to conducting an interview, so Lauren would have to do her typical intern duties of setting up the clothes and making sure they were presentable.

Lauren unloaded the clothes and then went looking for Kimball, who she found sitting on a couch with Natasha Bedingfield. Kimball introduced Lauren, and the two young women shook hands.

"You're my cell phone ring," Lauren told Natasha.

"Cool," Natasha said.

Kimball told Natasha that Lauren would be conducting the rest of the interview. Natasha suggested they go outside, because the weather was so lovely.

They sat down in some chairs out on the deck, and Kimball handed Lauren a little digital voice recorder. Lauren was nervous, but she was able to keep it in check. She told herself that it was going to be easy.

"How would you describe your personal style?" Lauren asked.

Kimball whispered in Lauren's ear to turn on the recorder. Oops. She did so, just as Natasha began answering the question. Natasha liked to mix vintage pieces with new things to achieve her personal look. When Lauren asked what Natasha's favorite piece of clothing was, Natasha thought for a moment and then said, "Probably a really good bra."

Lauren held in a laugh. She began to relax a little, feeling like she was getting the hang of interviewing someone.

As if to confirm the notion, Kimball whispered in her ear, "You're doing great." The rest of the interview was a breeze.

Honor Bright (Sort Of)

Heidi and Jordan

It was three days after New Year's Eve, and Heidi was still getting used to having a puppy. She loved Bella with all her heart, but it was a struggle to figure out how to take care of a dog and go to work and have time with Jordan. The balancing act wasn't easy. Sometimes one area suffered while she was paying attention to everything else.

The night Jordan gave Bella to Heidi had been such a special evening spent with Lauren and Jason. All four of the friends had felt very grown-up as they opened Christmas presents at Heidi and Lauren's apartment.

Bella getting up to no good!

Heidi had wanted a dog for as long she had lived in Los Angeles, and had been thrilled to receive Bella as a gift. But now, barely a week later, Heidi was wondering if having a dog was a good idea.

It was still early when Heidi had to get up out of bed and put on some clothes to take Bella for a walk. Every morning, for the past eight mornings, long before Heidi usually woke up, there was Bella, scratching at the door, begging to be taken outside.

Now, dressed in sweatpants and her bedhead partially hidden by a hairband, Heidi was waiting for her beautiful wonderful adorable bundle of puppy joy to take a dump.

"C'mon, Bella, be a good girl," she coaxed. "After you're done, we can go see Daddy," Heidi said, referring to Jordan.

Unfortunately, the walk around the courtyard continued without any puppy bowel movement success. As she followed Bella around, Heidi tried not to admit to herself that a dog—not just Bella, but any dog—might be too much to handle with the way her life was right now.

And then, in a moment that Heidi had felt sure was never going to occur that morning, Bella did her business, and it was time to go in. Thoughts about the appropriateness of dog ownership would have to wait.

Inside the apartment, Jordan was making eggs. Heidi was happy to see Jordan up; she hated leaving the apartment while he was asleep.

"So what are you and Bella going to do today?" she asked, as she helped herself to some eggs.

"Play, sleep, work out," Jordan said. And then he tentatively added, "Get a tattoo."

"You are not getting a tattoo, Jordan," Heidi said.

"We've been over this. It's a present from Lauren and Jason. If I don't get it, it'll be an insult to them," Jordan said. He knew it wasn't the best reason to get a tattoo, but he thought it might work well enough as a reason that morning.

"Think about when you're forty, and you'll have a tattoo," Heidi said.

"They'll have medicine to take it off, the way technology's going," Jordan replied.

Heidi rolled her eyes. "Where are you thinking of getting it?" she asked.

"There's this place up on Sunset that Jason knows about," he said.

"Where on your body?" Heidi clarified.

"On my back, on my shoulder," Jordan said.

Heidi looked at Jordan's back and tried to picture it with a tattoo. She wasn't pleased by the image.

"I don't think you should do it, Jordan," she said.

Bella jumped up onto Jordan's lap, trying to get at his eggs. "What if I get a tattoo of Bella—would it be okay then?" Jordan tried.

"No! No tattoo," Heidi said.

"I really want one, baby," Jordan pleaded. "I've been thinking about it for twenty-one years. When I was eight months old I started thinking about getting a tattoo," he said.

Heidi wasn't amused. She went into the bedroom to change clothes for work. Jordan looked down at Bella, who jumped up and tried to lick Jordan's nose. Then he began cleaning up the dishes from breakfast.

Heidi changed quickly and came out to find Jordan playing with Bella on the couch. Heidi was still upset at the idea of him getting a tattoo, but she had to admit that seeing her boyfriend and her new little puppy playing on the couch warmed her heart.

"I love you guys," she said, and bent down to kiss Jordan good-bye.

"We love you," Jordan said.

"No tattoo," Heidi said forcefully.

"OK," Jordan said, but he didn't look at Heidi and instead continued to play with Bella.

"Promise?" Heidi said.

"Promise," Jordan repeated.

"Honor bright?" Heidi asked. It was a term she and Jordan had been using since the beginning of their relationship. It was their version of telling the truth, an 'I cross my heart and hope to die' swear that meant something to both of them.

Jordan didn't reply. Heidi walked to the door and opened it. Before she left she said, "Daddy'll be in a lot of trouble if he has a tattoo when Mommy comes home from work."

"What if it's a tattoo of your name?" Jordan asked.

"No tattoo." The door shut with a thud.

Jordan looked at the dog. They both knew he was going to get a tattoo.

Like Robert De Niro in *Cape Fear*

Heidi

Heidi drove to work, still upset. She knew he was going to get the tattoo no matter what she said. It bothered her that he wouldn't talk it out with her. If he listened, really listened to what Heidi was saying, she was sure she could change his mind.

She pulled into the Bolthouse underground garage and parked her car. Walking up the ramp, Heidi couldn't get this tattoo business out of her mind. She had to be able to do something to stop it.

She walked into the office, on time for once. It was a new year, and this was the new, on-time Heidi, at least for today. Heidi's coworker Deb was already in, which meant that her dog, Rocket, would be there, too. Sure enough, Rocket ran up to say hello to Heidi. The dog was affectionate, and Heidi liked playing with him when she had nothing better to do at work. She looked forward to the day she could bring Bella into the office. Then Bella and Rocket could play together. But first, Heidi had to wait until Bella stopped peeing anywhere she felt like. Heidi knew Brent wouldn't want a dog peeing all over the office—who would?

Elodie came over to Heidi's desk to say hello.

"How was your Christmas?" Elodie asked.

"Good. I got a puppy from my boyfriend."

"Do you have a picture?"

Heidi handed over her cell phone to Elodie. Loaded onto it were a ton of shots of both Bella and Jordan.

"How is Jordan?" asked Elodie, when she scrolled past a picture of him on the phone.

"He's the cutest," Heidi said.

"You guys are so in love. I'm jealous," admitted Elodie.

"He wants to get a tattoo," Heidi said.

Elodie was surprised by the tattoo news. Jordan didn't seem the type. "Why does he want to get a tattoo?" she asked.

"'Cause Jason has one," Heidi replied.

"Where does he want to get it?" Elodie said.

"Some place on Sunset."

"I meant body part."

"Oh, that's so funny," said Heidi, laughing. "Jordan made that same mistake this morning. He wants to get it on his back."

As she talked to Elodie, Heidi was trying to get her computer to work, but the Internet connection kept failing. Elodie offered some advice on how to get the Internet hook-up working. Heidi tried it, and magically, she was online. She thanked Elodie and then the two girls walked into the kitchen to get their morning coffee.

"What's the tattoo going to be?" Elodie asked, as she poured them both coffee.

"He wants to get a cross with, like, scripture on the inside," Heidi said.

"Like in the middle of his back, like Robert DeNiro in *Cape Fear?*" Elodie asked.

"No, I don't think so. He's going to get it on his shoulder blade," Heidi said. "I really don't want him to get one."

"I know. He'll have it forever," Elodie said disapprovingly.

The girls took their coffees back to their desks. The workday was beginning, and Heidi already had things piling up on her desk. Worrying about Jordan's tattoo would have to take a backseat to work.

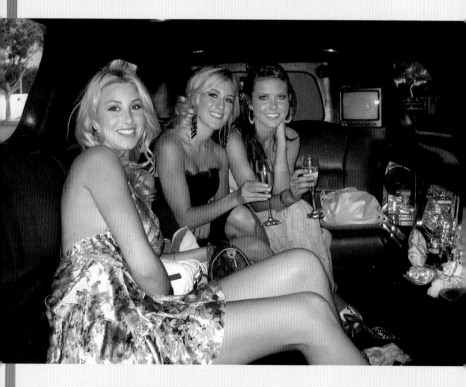

To Tattoo or Not to Tattoo

Jason and Jordan

Jordan and Jason enjoyed working out together. Each guy egged the other on as they lifted weights; there was a healthy sense of competition between the two of them that only made their workouts that much better.

The Emerson Gym in West Hollywood was their preferred location. It had a good mix of free weights and machines, and it wasn't a supersized mega-gym. Jordan didn't enjoy standing in lines to work out. Getting the motivation to lift weights three times a week was hard enough, but when you had to stand in line on top of that? That just wasn't a cool way to spend your time.

The morning rush was thankfully over by the time Jordan and Jason arrived. There were only two other guys in the room, which was great. Jordan picked up a dumbbell. "You want to do legs, lower back, calves, and shoulders?" he asked. Jordan was usually the one who kept track of which body parts they were exercising each day.

"Yeah, that sounds good," Jason said. "So, you gonna go through with the tattoo?"

Jordan picked up two dumbbells and started doing squats. "It was pandemonium this morning with Heidi," he said in response.

"She's not into it?" Jason said.

"No. She says she'll be pissed off at me for the rest of her life."

"That doesn't sound good," Jason said.

The guys continued with their workout, moving through their sets of squats on to sets of calf lifts. The lunges came next. Neither of the guys was a big fan of lunges, but they both knew they were better off doing them.

"Do you know what kind of tat you want to get?" Jason asked, as they neared the end of their third set of lunges.

"I was thinking *Thug Life* across my stomach with two guns," Jordan cracked. "Just get all tatted. Maybe a neck tattoo. That'd be sick. Heidi would flip."

After Jason stopped laughing, Jordan continued, "Actually, I was thinking about a cross on my shoulder blade."

"That sounds good," Jason said, and continued his last set of lunges.

The guys continued pumping iron for another half-hour. Afterward they were spent—completely tired from the workout. They left the gym and got into Jason's car.

"Let's get tatted," Jason said.

"Heidi's gonna flip," Jordan repeated, as they drove away in the car.

Inked

Jason and Jordan

Jason's car pulled up to the Shamrock Social Club, Hollywood's premier tattoo parlor. As they were getting out of the car, Jordan confessed, "I'm kinda nervous. Actually, I'm not nervous, I just—I just want to get it."

"They can be kind of addicting," said Jason, trying to fan the flames of Jordan's anxiety. "What did Heidi say in her text?"

On the way over, Heidi had been texting Jordan on his Sidekick. It had gone back and forth many times, with Jordan getting more annoyed with each text message.

"She said, or should I say, she wrote, 'Jordan, if you get one, I'm kicking you in the nuts.' "

"That's quite an incentive," Jason said sarcastically.

"She thinks I'm gonna wuss out," Jordan said, as they walked into the Shamrock.

The walls of the legendary tattoo parlor were covered with tattoo art. Crosses, flowers, stars, every animal imaginable, every design imaginable was represented in black line drawings on the walls. On the counter were books filled with even more drawings and photographs of tattoos.

There was a pool table in the front of the shop, for people to play on as they waited their turn to get inked. A row of seats lined one wall for the people who needed a rest before or after their tattoo session.

Jordan and Jason walked by the pool table and the row of seats, and headed straight for the counter. Mark Mahoney, the

proprietor, greeted them. Mark had slicked-back black hair that gave him the look of a rockabilly star.

"So, we're really doing it?" Jordan said to Jason. It hardly seemed real.

"I talked him into it," Jason explained to Mark with a conspiratorial air.

"Oh, so you're the bad influence," Mark said.

"I guess so," Jason replied, all too comfortable with the idea.

Mark asked them what kind of ink they were looking for that day.

"I want to get a cross on my right arm," Jason said.

"I want a cross, too, but on my back," Jordan said.

"Okay, so we'll crucify you guys here today," Mark said.

Jordan still felt nervous, but he and Jason started looking through the books of tattoo art to find just the right cross. Mark asked them if there was certain type of cross they wanted.

"I want one that has room inside for writing," Jordan said.

"What do you want to write in it?" asked Mark.

"It's the scripture my dad lives his life by—Jeremiah 29:11," Jordan said. " 'For I know the plans I have for you,' declares the Lord. 'Plans to prosper you and not to harm you, plans to give you hope and a future.' "

"Wow," said Jason. "Those are some pretty deep words."

"I know," said Jordan. "It has a lot of meaning to my dad and to me."

"So you want it to read, *Jeremiah 29:11*?" asked Mark.

"Yeah, that's what I want," Jordan said.

"I think Heidi's gonna like it. It's meaningful, you know?" Jason said.

The guys kept browsing through the books for just the right design. Mark made a few suggestions, and eventually Jordan and Jason each found the kind of cross they wanted.

Mark took them into the back room, where the actual tattooing was done. There were three workstations, where the tattoo artists applied their trade. One wall was lined with mirrors, and the other had windows so that you could see what a lovely day it was outside while you had needles applied to your flesh.

"So, are you nervous?" Mark asked, as the guys entered the back room.

"I'm looking forward to it," Jason replied.

"You," Mark said, pointing to Jordan, "you're nervous."

"Maybe a little," Jordan admitted.

"It's OK, man," Mark said.

The guys sat down on the stools at the workstations. Mark was going to do Jason's tattoo and Andrew, another tattoo artist, was going to work on Jordan. Mark began shaving the area on Jason's arm where the tattoo would go with a blue disposable razor. Andrew did the same to Jordan's back. There wasn't a lot of talking.

After the shaving was done, a dark line transfer of the cross Jordan wanted was put on his back and then rubbed. The transfer was removed, and Jordan got to see the drawing of the cross on his back. These transfers allowed the artist to have a guide as he did the inking, and it gave Jordan a good idea of what the tattoo was going to look like on his skin when it was done. Jordan liked the way it looked. Jason looked over from his stool and nodded approvingly.

When the actual tattooing began, it wasn't painful really, more uncomfortable, and Jordan soon got used to it. Jason had felt the sting of the tattoo needle before and took it all in stride.

Then Jordan's Sidekick started vibrating on the table next to him. He couldn't reach it because he was getting the tattoo, but he knew who it was.

"I ain't trying to answer that," he said with a drawl.

The tattoo artists continued their work silently. *So this is what a tattoo feels like*, thought Jordan. He couldn't help but wonder what Heidi would say when she saw it.

Size Matters

Audrina

Along Franklin Avenue in Hollywood, just east of Vine, is a little row of shops. This strip of stores is just a block long, but it brings the whole area to life. There is a coffeehouse, a bookstore, a theater, and four restaurants. La Poubelle is one of the restaurants along that strip, and it was there that Audrina and Shannon had decided to go on their first date after meeting over the chocolate cupcake a few days before.

It was a French restaurant, but very casual, with delicious food. Audrina and Shannon got a table by the front window. There were three small candles flickering on the table, and it all felt very romantic.

Shannon had picked up Audrina at her apartment after work. He held the door for her as she got in his car, and Audrina liked being treated that way. The ride to the restaurant took only fifteen minutes, but in that time Audrina felt herself growing closer to Shannon already.

When they were seated in the restaurant, Audrina decided it was going to be a good evening. She ordered the filet mignon, and Shannon went with the *crêpes poulet*. The waiter brought their drinks and put two straws down on the table. Shannon picked his up. It was an odd malformed straw, roughly the thickness of a toothpick.

"This is the tiniest straw I have ever seen," he said with a laugh.

"You don't like straws, huh?" Audrina said.

"Not skinny ones," Shannon said.

Audrina held up her regular-sized straw.

"My straw is bigger than yours," she joked.

"You're going to give me a complex about that now," Shannon said.

The food soon arrived as well as a new straw for Shannon. The evening was going along smoothly. Shannon was one of the nicest guys she had met in a long, long time. They decided to walk to the coffeehouse down the block for dessert. When the bill came, Shannon told Audrina that his band was going on tour next month, and he'd be gone for two months. Audrina was taken

aback. It was too early to know what was going to happen between the two of them, but the tour definitely threw a monkey
wrench into her visions of the future.

"Can I see you rehearse sometime?" she asked. If Shannon
was leaving next month Audrina decided they should make the
most of the time they had together now. As they walked out of
the restaurant, Audrina suggested they skip the coffee shop and
head back to her place for dessert instead. Shannon gave her a
slow smile and said he'd like nothing better.

Not the Reaction He Was Hoping For

Lauren, Heidi, Jason, and Jordan

It was dark by the time Jordan and Jason left the Shamrock
Social Club. On the drive back to the apartment, Jordan was
feeling good, and the slight sting of the tattoo couldn't take that
feeling away. Jordan could see now why Jason had said tattoos
can be addicting. He suspected this wouldn't be the only tattoo
he got in his life.

Jason was also feeling good. He was looking forward to seeing Lauren after a long day apart. Jason didn't mention Heidi to
Jordan on the drive back to the girls' apartment. If Jordan

wanted to bring up his girlfriend or what her reaction to the tattoo might be, that was up to Jordan. They drove in contemplative silence.

Inside Lauren and Heidi's apartment, the girls were sitting on the couch with Bella jumping all over them playfully. Lauren knew that Jason was getting a tattoo that day, and Heidi knew that Jordan went with him, but they still didn't know if Jordan had actually gone through with it.

"What if he got *Heidi* across his chest?" Lauren asked.

"I'd be, like, 'Nice, that's my name; don't wear it out,' " Heidi said. The girls giggled.

Jordan and Jason knocked on the door and then walked into the apartment. Jordan didn't make eye contact with Heidi.

Lauren, for her part, was excited to see Jason's new tattoo. "Come on; let's see it," she said to Jason.

Jason rolled up his sleeve and revealed the white bandage covering the tattoo.

Heidi said to Jordan, "I don't think you got anything. Honor bright, you didn't get one."

Jason removed his bandage, and Lauren took one look at it and declared, "I love it." Heidi didn't say anything.

"That looks so cool," Jordan said.

Without any prompting, Jordan began to take off his shirt. Heidi spotted the bandage on Jordan's back, but she still couldn't believe Jordan would actually do this, not after "honor bright."

"No you didn't. Hush your mouth," she said.

Heidi stood up to take a closer look at the bandage. She pulled up one corner slowly and sneaked a peek underneath.

"It is not real," she said stubbornly.

"It is, baby," Jordan said, as he pulled off the entire bandage.

Heidi stood there looking at Jordan's new real tattoo. "Oh my god, it's real," she whispered, as the truth sank in.

Lauren told Jordan that she liked it, and Jordan thanked her. Heidi sank back down on the couch with Bella in her arms.

"I am so mad at you, Jordan Patrick Eubanks. You think this tattoo is gonna make you a badass now?" Heidi fumed.

Jordan didn't reply. Even though he knew Heidi wouldn't like the tattoo initially, he'd hoped she might warm up to it once she saw it. Holding Bella close to her, Heidi said, "We don't like you anymore." Then Heidi and Bella went into the bedroom and closed the door.

Still Not Happy

Heidi and Audrina

Her apartment complex was a wonderful place to live, as far as Heidi was concerned. It had everything—great apartments, a pool, a gym, and it was close to a lot of her favorite restaurants. Tonight, it was all about the gym. Heidi worked out a lot, but since starting work at Bolthouse, finding the time to do it was getting more and more difficult. Luckily for Heidi, Audrina was in a similar situation, working full-time at Quixote Studios, so they made the perfect workout partners.

Heidi and Audrina entered the gym and headed for the treadmills, finding two empty machines side by side.

"Mine says *error*. I don't think it's working. All right, I'm done working out," said Heidi sarcastically.

"Try pushing start," Audrina advised.

Heidi's machine jerked into motion, making her stumble. "Uh-oh, almost had a wardrobe malfunction there," she said as she adjusted her top.

"Did I tell you Jason convinced Jordan to get a tattoo?" Heidi said. "He was a virgin and now he's already talking about a second one."

"I hear they can be addicting," Audrina said. "What's it of?"

"A cross, on his shoulder blade."

Heidi pressed a button on the treadmill that made it incline, so now she was walking uphill. "This is good for the gluteus maximus," she said.

"What's he want for his next one?" Audrina asked.

"He wants praying hands. Which I guess is better than a devil's tongue, or something crazy." Heidi said.

"I want to stop; I'm getting strep throat," Heidi said nonsensically, and turned off the treadmill. Any excuse to stop working out. Audrina finished up on the treadmill soon after.

The girls walked over to the free weights area.

"You know the only thing I do in the weight room is weigh myself?" Heidi said. She got on the scales, looked at the number, made a funny face, and stepped off.

Audrina picked up the twelve-pound dumbbells while Heidi grabbed the five-pounders.

"I think Jason is a bad influence on Jordan," said Heidi.

"Seriously?" said Audrina as she curled the dumbbell.

"No, I just wish Jordan didn't get the tattoo."

"Does he know you don't like it?" Audrina asked.

"I pretended to be mad at him, but it wore off," Heidi said. She sighed as she continued to lift weights. Being an understanding girlfriend was hard work.

Cheer Bear's Big Adventure

Heidi and Jordan

Heidi had left most of her Care Bear collection back in Colorado, moving to Los Angeles with just two of them, True Heart Bear and Cheer Bear. She loved those bears beyond reason. But now, tragedy had struck: Cheer Bear was missing. Heidi had looked over the entire apartment twice, but Cheer Bear was nowhere to be found.

Heidi had had her beloved Cheer Bear for at least five years, and she couldn't believe it was just gone. What could have happened to it? She called Jordan, who said he hadn't seen the bear in a few days, but promised Heidi that he'd help her look for it when he got home.

Heidi inspected Bella for signs that the dog had been chewing on a stuffed bear, but Bella showed no indication of having used poor innocent Cheer Bear as a chew toy. Heidi then called Lauren, who hadn't seen it either. She made Lauren call Jason with the odd request, "You didn't put Heidi's Care Bear somewhere, did you?" Jason replied that he didn't even know Heidi *had* a Care Bear.

As she searched everywhere, Heidi felt like her childhood hero, girl detective Nancy Drew, but she had to admit she had run out of clues.

The next day Heidi went to work, still upset about her lost stuffed bear. After she left, Jordan made a trip to the dry cleaners, where he picked up a box. Inside the box was Cheer Bear, looking and smelling as good as new. He took the bear home and put it on Heidi's bed. Then Jordan called Heidi to tell her that he found Cheer Bear behind the bed. Heidi was so happy she screamed, "Thank you! I love you, Jordan."

Jordan was relieved. Two days earlier, he had come home and found that Bella had peed on Cheer Bear. Jordan knew Heidi would completely freak out if she discovered what Bella had done, so he hid the bear in his backpack and took it to the dry cleaners the next day. The dry cleaners did an excellent job—there was no stain or smell left on the bear.

Heidi came home that night and was overjoyed to be re-united with Cheer Bear. Jordan was happy, too, satisfied that he had saved Heidi from finding out that her dog had almost ruined her favorite stuffed animal. Three cheers for Cheer Bear!

Heidi's Favorite Care Bears

1. True Heart Bear

2. Cheer Bear

3. Love-a-Lot Bear

4. Tenderheart Bear

5. Laugh-a-Lot Bear

All You Need Is Love— And Antibiotics

Heidi and Audrina

Three weeks after getting Bella, Heidi realized something was wrong with her dog. Bella was already way too big for a teacup Chihuahua. Heidi had a feeling that Jordan had been lied to by the dog-sellers. There was also the problem of all the peeing. Heidi never would have dreamed a dog could go to the bathroom so often. Bella was becoming a much larger responsibility than Heidi could have imagined, but she didn't want to admit it. Besides growing too fast and peeing too much, the dog was looking sickly and tired. The only thing to do was to take her to the vet.

The veterinarian's waiting room was a large space with wide chairs. Heidi took a seat opposite a woman with a sick cockatoo. While Heidi was waiting for the vet, a small worm came out of Bella's butt and landed on Heidi's leg. *Oh my god.* Heidi thought she was going to throw up, but she held it together. When Heidi's number was called, she and Bella went into the examination room.

The vet did a thorough examination of Bella and then told Heidi the bad news. Bella had worms, most likely two or three kinds. The vet prescribed some pills to give the dog over the next three weeks. The vet also confirmed Heidi's suspicion that Bella wasn't a teacup Chihuahua. She was just a regular-size Chihuahua.

On the way home from the vet's office, Heidi reflected that

just maybe buying a dog without papers, through Craigslist, in a parking lot, from a shady guy from Fresno, might not have been the smartest thing Jordan had ever done.

Heidi got back to the apartment and went directly to Audrina's with Bella. Audrina let her in, and then Heidi told her the tale of the worms and how Bella wasn't even a teacup Chihuahua.

"Sounds like Jordan got screwed over," said Audrina.

When Bella was a puppy, she was smaller than Heidi's stuffed Chihuahua!

"Totally," said Heidi. "And the vet thinks Bella might have been abused, too." Heidi was almost crying at this point; the situation was so overwhelming. "It's a lot of responsibility. I wanted a dog, but I never would have bought one for myself," Heidi said, as tears rolled down her cheeks.

Audrina wasn't sure what to say. She put her arm around her friend to comfort her.

"I really love Bella, but if she pees on my bed one more time, I don't know what I'm going to do," Heidi cried.

"Heidi, it's just a little cute dog. All you have to do is love it and put down some newspaper," Audrina said reasonably.

Audrina offered to help Heidi train the dog, and Heidi felt relieved by the kind offer. The entire day had been bad news, and Heidi still didn't know what she was going to do, but she felt better knowing that Audrina would help. That was what having good friends was all about.

Looking Forward to Valentine's Day

Lauren, Heidi, and Audrina

Valentine's Day was just around the corner, and Lauren and Heidi still had a lot to do. The girls had decided to make their own cards for their boyfriends this year. But it was a beautiful day in Southern California, and the girls decided to first get some sun. They called Audrina to see if she was up for some tanning; she said she'd meet them by the pool.

The pool wasn't crowded and the girls had their choice of the prime spots. After making sure they were wearing the appropriate amount of suntan lotion, the girls moved three lounge chairs together and sat back to relax.

Audrina was curious about what the girls did last Valentine's Day.

"I don't like Valentine's Day," Lauren said. "Last year I watched recorded episodes of *The O.C.* I've never had a good Valentine's Day."

"That's gonna change this year," Heidi said confidently.

"What about you, Heidi?" Audrina asked.

"It was just drama last year; I don't want to think about it," Heidi said with a wave of her hand. "What about you?"

"I didn't do anything," Audrina said.

"Well, it's good you have a valentine now," Heidi said.

"Do you know what you're getting Jordan?" Audrina asked.

"I got him this cross with black diamonds on it. He's gonna love it. He'll probably cry when he sees it," Heidi said.

"I'm making this memory box for Jason that will hold all our photos and stuff," Lauren said. "What are you doing for Shannon?"

The girls all turned over on their stomachs so their backs could soak up some of the sun.

"He's going on tour soon, so I got him some shaving stuff that he can take with him, and he likes to read, so I got him this cool *Did You Know* book. I wanted to make him a cupcake, but I don't have any time because of work."

"We could make it for you," Lauren offered.

"Seriously? That would be great," Audrina said. "It's chocolate with chocolate frosting. You know, we met at that café when we shared a cupcake."

"That is so romantic," Heidi said.

"Consider it done. Do you want to put it in a box or anything?" Lauren asked.

Audrina mulled it over. "Maybe a red or pink box with a ribbon on it," she said.

Heidi and Lauren promised to make it happen.

With that resolved, all three girls were convinced they were going to have a great Valentine's Day for a change.

Do You Believe in a Thing Called Love? Roses, Violins, and Romance

Lauren: Not a romantic person, but believes when you meet the right guy, romance can bloom. Likes getting fun, quirky gifts like a huge, swirly lollipop instead of flowers.

Whitney: Romance exists in so many forms—anyone who doesn't believe in it is a pessimist.

Audrina: Believes in love at first sight, and believes a great relationship must have trust, communication, and honesty.

Heidi: Romance is the most important thing in the world. Her fairy-tale date was when Jordan took her horseback riding and set up a gorgeous picnic.

Isn't It Romantic?

Jason and Jordan

Standing proudly on a corner of Sunset Boulevard is the infamous Hustler Store. Located in the heart of the Sunset Strip, the Hustler Store is, not surprisingly, a beacon for all things

Hustler. Jason and Jordan thought it might be amusing to shop there for Valentine's Day gifts for their girlfriends.

Inside the air-conditioned store, Jason and Jordon leisurely perused the aisles. They hadn't come in with any concrete idea about what it was they were looking for exactly. They began arguing over whose idea it had been to go into the store in the first place. Jason claimed it was Jordan who'd had the bright idea of visiting a store that sells pornography and sex toys, but Jordan was of the belief that Jason had masterminded the whole thing. Jordan pointed out that Jason had been the one driving, to which Jason had no response.

"Maybe they have perverted candy hearts Heidi might like," Jordan said.

"What about these sexual fantasy vouchers?" Jason said, reading one aloud, "I owe you one kinky striptease."

"Why, thank you," Jordan said, mock-flirtatiously.

Surrounded by candy-colored edible panties and fur-lined handcuffs, the boys didn't know where to begin.

"I keep gravitating to this lube," Jordan said, trying not to laugh.

"Nothing says *I Love You* like lubricant," Jason cracked.

"What are your plans for Valentine's Day anyway?" Jordan asked.

"In the morning I'm sending her flowers. And then a car is going to pick us up and we'll spend the day at this cool spa I found. Then we'll have a nice quiet dinner. And just hang out."

Jordan was impressed that Jason had planned what sounded like a wonderful day for Lauren.

"What do you have going on?" Jason asked, walking past a life-size blow-up doll.

"We're going horseback riding, and then we're going to have a sunset picnic in Griffith Park near the Hollywood sign," Jordan said.

"That sounds killer."

"Yeah, Heidi used to train horses when she was a kid," Jordan said. He was proud of himself for coming up with the idea and was confident Heidi would have a great time.

Jason finally picked up a box of candy hearts that he thought Lauren might like. On the way out of the store, Jordan spotted something. On the table by the door was a stack of boxes. Jordan moved closer to inspect them. He held up one of the boxes for Jason to see.

"These are heart-shaped chocolate thongs," Jordan said.

"To wear?" Jason asked.

Jordan nodded.

"No way."

"I've never seen anything like these before," Jordan said.

"Does chocolate even belong down there?" Jason wondered.

"I don't think I want to find out," Jordan said.

"Let's not tell the girls we came here," Jason said.

It was the best idea Jordan had heard all day.

Shakespeare Was Never Her Best Subject

Lauren and Heidi

Inside Lauren and Heidi's apartment, the roommates were sitting on the floor, tearing out pictures from magazines. The pictures were for the Valentine's Day cards they had finally gotten around to starting.

Heidi missed Audrina, but their friend had had to go into work late that day, which was the only reason she had been out sunning with them earlier. As Heidi paged through the magazine, trying to find just the right picture of two people kissing to use for her card, she thought back to the Valentine's Days she had experienced growing up. In Colorado everyone in her family would make a valentine for everyone else, and then they would all sneak around and put the cards in bags hanging on the bedroom doorknobs. It was so much fun. In the morning, even if it was a school day, Heidi's mom would make heart-shaped pancakes.

Meanwhile, Lauren looked for the right image to put on her card for Jason. Lauren told everyone she hated Valentine's Day, but she did like remembering when she was in elementary school and she would get valentines from everyone in the class. Those were such sweet little valentine cards, with *To Lauren* written at the top of all of them.

"I don't know how I'm going to do this exactly," Heidi said, interrupting Lauren's thoughts.

"What are you planning on doing with yours?" Lauren asked.

"I'm going to cut out a big red heart and put it between these two pictures of me and Jordan and then I'm going to add pictures of sunsets and hearts from magazines," she said. "Do we have scissors?"

"We have, like, three pairs. I just don't know where they are," Lauren replied.

She got up and found a pair in the kitchen. She held them up for Heidi.

"I have these," she said. They were red toy scissors that Bella played with.

"Didn't we have a purple pair?" Heidi asked.

Lauren walked into Heidi's room and found the purple scissors in the bathroom. She brought them into the living room and handed them to Heidi, who began cutting up the pictures she had selected from the magazine.

"I also wrote him this poem at work. I was bored, so I wrote a poem. It's in bionic pentameter," Heidi said. She'd remembered the term from high school English class.

"Bionic pentameter?" Lauren repeated.

"You know, like, ten syllables per line," Heidi said.

"I think that's *iambic* pentameter," Lauren said.

"I guess I get my pentameters mixed up sometimes," Heidi said, laughing.

Lauren taped Hershey's Kisses to her card and held it up for Heidi to see. "My card is edible. What does your card do?"

"I was gonna do that, too," Heidi said.

"Copycat," Lauren laughed.

The girls went back to cutting pictures and taping kisses and sweetheart candies to their cards.

Taking Care of Business

Jason and Jordan

"I want to get a bouquet of flowers," Jason said to the woman behind the counter. Jason and Jordan had driven to The Velvet Garden on Third Street. It was Jason's favorite florist.

"Can I see some arrangements to get an idea of what I want?" he requested.

The woman took Jason and Jordan to the back part of the shop, where the flowers were stored. The women in the back of the store were working at a feverish pace. It was the day before Valentine's Day, and they had hundreds of orders that needed to go out. The woman from the counter wanted to know what Jason's girlfriend's favorite flowers were. Jason knew the answer but had forgotten their name.

"They're white and grow on a bush," he said.

"Does that narrow it down enough for you?" Jordan asked sarcastically.

"There's lots of them on a bush, and they smell," Jason said, floundering.

"Gardenias?" she asked.

"That's it," Jason said, relieved. "I want a big bouquet of roses and gardenias."

Jordan started doubting if Heidi was going to like the horses and the picnic he had planned. Maybe he should have done a spa like Jason. Jordan calmed his doubts by reminding himself that Heidi loved horses and wandered back to the front of the store.

Jason thought that it smelled like spring in that back room

with all the flowers. He looked around at the different arrangements and decided on one he liked.

At the front counter, after he'd paid for the arrangement, Jason asked the woman to write the card for him.

"My handwriting is a little shaky," he explained. "Can you write, *Happy Valentine's Day. A fun day awaits you. Love, Jason.*"

Jordan leaned on the counter and said, "You know, Lauren was saying a couple days ago, she's never had a good Valentine's Day."

"That's all changing tomorrow," Jason said confidently.

"That was a pretty sweet setup," Jordan commented, as they exited the florist.

"They handle all my flower business," joked Jason. Jordan laughed, and they headed out into the night.

Lauren's Five Favorite Romantic Things That Jason Does

1. Breakfast in bed

2. Any time he cooks for me

3. He leaves and then comes back two minutes later to give me a kiss because he misses me already.

4. Lots of little things mean more to me than some big present.

5. He gives me flowers.

The Best Valentine's Day Ever

Lauren, Heidi, Jason, and Jordan

On the morning of Valentine's Day, Lauren was sitting on the floor, putting some final chocolate kisses on the card she had made for Jason, when the doorbell rang. Lauren got up to answer the door. A delivery guy asked if she was Lauren. She said she was, and he handed her a gigantic bouquet of gardenias accented with a dozen roses. Lauren could barely carry it. She placed it on the table in the living room.

The flowers were amazing. They made the whole apartment smell like spring. Ever since she was a little girl in Laguna Beach, gardenias had been her favorite. Growing up, her house always had flowers in it. And when her mother brought home gardenias, Lauren loved them the most. The ones Jason had sent over were exquisite. Their creamy white flowers brightened the whole room.

Heidi ran in from her bedroom to see them. She was impressed by the sheer size of the arrangement. Heidi knew what Jason had planned for Lauren that day, but she hadn't said anything. Heidi wanted Lauren to be surprised, but when she saw the flowers, she couldn't help but hint that she knew what was in store.

"You know what, this day might change your whole view on Valentine's Day," Heidi said playfully.

"Possibly," said Lauren, smiling.

Heidi went back into her room and finished up her own

Valentine's Day preparations. Heidi had devised a treasure hunt for Jordan. All around the apartment complex, Heidi had planted little notes that were clues for Jordan to figure out. Each note led to another, until finally they brought Jordan back to Heidi's apartment. There on her bed would be the four-foot card she had made and tons of valentine candy and a giant red teddy bear. As Heidi finished arranging the candies on the bed, the doorbell rang. It was Jordan! She left her bedroom and closed the door so Jordan couldn't peek in before he embarked on his treasure hunt.

When Heidi let Jordan in, he kissed her, and said loudly, "Happy Valentine's Day, baby." Heidi brought over her present for Jordan. It was the poem she had written in 'bionic' pentameter at work. Heidi had burned the edges of the paper and then rolled it in dry coffee and wrinkled it to make it look really old. She handed the ancient-looking document to Jordan, who inspected it skeptically.

"Did you burn the edges of this?" he asked.

"No, it's just really, really old," Lauren said sarcastically, as she walked out of her bedroom.

Jordan didn't quite know what to think of the poem. As he was about to start reading it, Heidi impatiently snatched it back from him.

"Want me to read it to you?" she asked.

"Yeah, sure," he said.

Heidi read in a loud clear voice, "Today is the day of love and hope,/for all those alone you hope they don't mope./This is only the beginning of our love,/when we're together I could float like a dove./Your love gets me through all those days and nights./Especially when we have those bad fights./Together forever is what we'll be./With you by my side, I could part the sea./You mean more to me than words could tell,/when I met you I was put in a spell./When you look at me, my heart always melts,/my heart beats so fast it forms welts./Price is the love we endure,/it's time for you to go on a tour."

Jordan was blown away. He loved it. More importantly, he loved that Heidi had spent so much time on something so thoughtful for him.

Now it was time for the treasure hunt to begin. Heidi gave Jordan his first clue. It was a little piece of paper that told Jordan to head to the laundry room. Jordan had no idea where any of this was headed, but he was happy to play along with Heidi. It was Valentine's Day after all, so why not indulge his girlfriend's crazy romantic ideas?

Jordan kissed Heidi good-bye and yelled a good-bye to Lauren, who had gone back into her room. Heidi closed the door behind Jordan and said, "Well, we won't see him for an hour and a half."

Lauren came back into the living room. "Where are you making him go, Heidi?"

"It's just a treasure hunt around the complex," Heidi said,

defending her kooky plan. "Now I have more time to make the treasure prize even prettier."

All in all, Heidi had placed clues in eighteen different spots throughout the complex. Jordan didn't know it yet, but he was going to be crisscrossing the area at least nine times. Heidi had made sure that each clue led to another clue that was as far away as possible.

At that moment Jordan was on his way to the laundry room, trying to understand what a treasure hunt had to do with Valentine's Day. Oh well. If Heidi wanted to express her love for him in this manner, he wasn't going to complain about it.

In the laundry room along one wall were three washing machines, and along the opposite wall were six dryers. Jordan looked around but didn't see any more clues. He even looked inside the washing machines, but still had no luck. He tried the dryers; the outcome was the same. There was a small folding table and he looked under that. Nothing.

Jordan looked around the room again. Could Heidi have meant another laundry room? Each floor had an identical laundry, as Jordan had discovered one day when all the washing machines were being used on Heidi's floor. On top of one of the dryers Jordan saw an empty mini box of detergent. He reached for it and there, written on the side of the box, was Heidi's handwriting: *In the gym you will find another lovely clue of mine.* Heidi wasn't going to make it easy. He took off for the gym, which was all the way on the other side of the complex.

Jordan started running. He didn't know how many clues there would be, but knowing Heidi, there would probably be a lot. Jordan had planned for the horseback riding to happen a little later in the day, but he didn't want to take any chances and be late because that would throw off the picnic plans.

Meanwhile, back in the apartment, Heidi placed more chocolates on her elaborate card. The prize at the end of the treasure hunt was now very, very chocolaty. Heidi's bed looked like a small candy store that only sold Valentine's Day candies. Lauren came in to take a final look at Heidi's creation.

"I think the teddy bear is what he's really going to like," said Lauren.

"Not the card?" said Heidi.

"He'll like the card, too, Heidi," Lauren assured her.

Heidi went back to arranging the prize. Lauren walked into the living room and reread the note that had come with her flowers. *A day of fun.* What did that mean? She knew Jason had been planning something for a while. He had been making secretive phone calls that ended abruptly when Lauren walked in. Jason didn't normally do stuff like that, so she knew he must have been formulating a plan.

Just then the doorbell rang. Lauren opened the door to find her boyfriend standing there with a big smile on his face.

"I think you're going to like today a lot," Jason said, and gave her a long kiss.

The day is already going pretty well, thought Lauren.

"We're going to a spa for the whole day, both of us," Jason said. "I found a private place in Beverly Hills where I think we can have some fun."

So that's what he'd meant by fun. Lauren loved the idea of going to a spa with Jason. She usually got pampered alone, when Jason was out of town. She assumed the spa day was the total of her Valentine's Day gift, but then Jason pulled out a small red gift-wrapped box he had been hiding behind his back. Lauren carefully untied the bow and unwrapped the box, then removed the lid. Inside were two beautiful diamond bracelets.

"Oh my god, they're beautiful. Thank you so much," Lauren said, as she threw her arms around Jason and hugged him. "I love them."

Jason just smiled.

"Why two?" Lauren asked.

"I couldn't make up my mind," Jason said.

Lauren kissed him again. She went into her bedroom and got out the gigantic card she had made Jason, as well as the memory box, which she had wrapped in pretty paper. Then she presented both of them to Jason. She wasn't sure what he would think of them, but as soon as he started reading the card, he smiled. On the card were pictures of Lauren and Jason kissing and holding hands. Jason gave Lauren another long kiss.

"I love it," he said.

Then Jason tore off the wrapping paper on the memory box. Inside the box were more pictures of Lauren and Jason, and also little love notes they had written each other. Jason was obviously moved. He hugged Lauren tightly and told her how much he loved the memory box and how much it meant to him.

Lauren and Jason said good-bye to Heidi and left for their day of spa fun. Heidi was impressed by Jason's presents. She knew Jason was getting Lauren a bracelet; she just hadn't expected to see two of them! *Only Jason would do something so elaborate,* thought Heidi.

The entire treasure hunt only took Jordan an hour and fifteen minutes to complete. He came back to the apartment looking for Heidi, but couldn't find her. He opened her bedroom door with the plan of calling her name, but before he could he caught sight of his treasure hunt prize. On the bed were the huge teddy bear, tons of candy, and the enormous card Heidi had made. Heidi jumped out from behind the bed.

"Surprise!" she yelled. Jordan hugged and kissed her.

Jordan read the card Heidi had made him and then kissed her again. He told her he had an exciting day planned, but it wouldn't begin for a couple of hours. Heidi wondered what they were going to do with no one else in the apartment and all that time on their hands.

"I'll think of something," Jordan said, and kissed her. Heidi was right. This was the best Valentine's Day ever, and it had only just begun.

The Best Valentine's Day Ever, Part Two

Lauren, Heidi, Jason, and Jordan

At the small exclusive Beverly Hills spa, Lauren and Jason felt like the only people in the world as they lay on side-by-side tables getting massages. It was so calming, and just what Lauren needed. She was so glad she didn't have work or school that day.

Meanwhile, on the edge of Griffith Park, Jordan and Heidi were approaching the horse rental stables.

"Oh my gosh, are you taking me horseback riding?" Heidi squealed. Jordan nodded. Heidi was so excited that she started jumping up and down.

"My dad always said the way to a girl's heart is with a horse," she babbled. "It's like you brought some of Colorado home for me. Thank you so much."

As they rode along the horse trail, Heidi told Jordan how she had had a fantasy of riding horses with him. "Jordan Patrick

Dining out at a favorite sushi joint.

Eubanks, you're my Prince Charming." Jordan leaned over on his horse to plant a kiss on Heidi.

"I've got one more surprise for you," he said mysteriously.

Heidi was dying to know what it was, but Jordan wouldn't tell her. She'd have to wait and see.

The horseback riding took Jordan and Heidi into beautiful parts of Griffith Park that Heidi didn't even know existed. As they handed the horses back over to the trainer, Heidi bid farewell to her lovely horse and gave Jordan a kiss. She told him again how much she loved the horseback riding and how special it was that she got to share it with him.

Heidi assumed they were driving home after that, but to her surprise, Jordan turned the car north.

"Where are we going?" she asked.

"You'll see," he said cryptically.

Soon Jordan pulled the car into a parking lot he had discovered a few weeks ago. It was high up in the hills, looking down on the city. Heidi and Jordan got out of the car. Jordan opened the trunk and pulled out a king-size picnic basket.

"I love picnics," Heidi said with delight.

"Then I think you're gonna love this," Jordan said.

"We don't have to hike, do we? You know I hate hiking," she said.

"It's more like a little walk," Jordan assured her, as he started walking toward an almost hidden path. Jordan had scoped out the picnic spot a few weeks earlier. It was secluded and had a wonderful view of the city, and the Hollywood sign was so big behind them you felt like you could almost reach out and touch it.

After the short walk, Jordan spread out the blanket he had brought and opened the picnic basket. Heidi was again blown away. Inside were all of Heidi's favorite foods—Manchego cheese, prosciutto, baguettes, and grapes. Jordan really had paid attention, which made the whole thing extra special.

"You are the cutest boy, and this is the best Valentine's Day I could have ever imagined," Heidi said.

Even after all that, Jordan had one more surprise for Heidi. He pulled out a ring box and handed it to her. Heidi was in shock. She opened the box, and inside was a ring encircled with diamonds. Heidi was so moved she almost cried.

"Oh my gosh, I love it. I love you," she said.

"I love you too, baby," Jordan said. He explained that it was a promise ring, "a promise that our love will stand strong forever."

Heidi embraced Jordan, and they kissed tenderly. Behind them the Hollywood sign, because of the setting sun's reflection, seemed to be glowing. They continued holding each other as they looked out at the magnificent view of the city that they now called home.

Better than Tacos

Whitney

Steak and potatoes was Whitney's favorite meal. She had always loved it, even as a kid. Whitney was big on texture, and for some reason the texture of the meat with the potatoes just felt right.

Her boyfriend, David, knew she liked steakhouses, and for Valentine's Day he had decided to take her to one of her favorites: a place in Hollywood called Sterling Steakhouse. He didn't tell Whitney of his plans, though, wanting it to be a surprise.

David picked Whitney up at her apartment just off campus near USC. She had no idea where David was taking her. He had just arrived at her door with an enormous bouquet of flowers and announced that they were going out. Whitney knew there was a party going on at a friend's house near campus, and she wondered if that was where they were going. It seemed a little early for a party—it was only 7:30 P.M.—and Whitney had heard the party was only for people who didn't have a valentine. That wasn't Whitney this year, and she was happy about it. But she still thought it might be fun to go to the party because so many of her friends from school were going to be there.

They got in the car and headed toward Hollywood—Whitney had spent her whole life in Los Angeles, so she knew that much. She and David both knew the quickest ways to get around the city, and this was a route to Hollywood that she recognized. But where in Hollywood was he taking her?

David was all smiles, but he wasn't giving up his surprise.

Whitney wasn't going to guess specific places, because if she was right, it might hurt David's feelings.

As they pulled onto Ivar Avenue and the sign to Sterling Steakhouse came into view, Whitney knew that had to be their destination. She hugged David and said, "Shut *up*! I love, love, love this place. Thank you so much."

The valet took David's keys, and they went inside. David had called ahead and made sure that everything was waiting just as he had planned. On their table were flowers matching the ones he had brought to the apartment. Whitney couldn't believe he'd gone to so much effort.

Whitney ordered the New York cut with mashed potatoes (her favorite), and David got the same. After the waiter left, Whitney handed David her Valentine's Day present. David had just begun studying music in one of his classes, and Whitney had decided to give him some of her favorite music that she thought he might like—the Beatles *Anthology* CD. David loved it, and thanked Whitney with a kiss.

It was turning into the best Valentine's Day Whitney had ever had.

Whitney's Favorite Restaurants in Los Angeles

1. Ruth's Chris Steakhouse
2. In-N-Out Burger
3. Reddi Chick
4. Zen Zoo
5. Cecil's Barbeque
6. Brent's Deli
7. Sterling Steakhouse
8. Cynthia's
9. Pane Fresco
10. Taiko

Low-Key Romance

Audrina

Audrina came home from work as early as possible on Valentine's Day. She had given her spare apartment key to Heidi so that Heidi could drop off the cupcake before she went out with Jordan.

All day long at work, Audrina had been thinking about that cupcake. She opened the door to her apartment, and there on the kitchen counter was a red gift-wrapped box with a white bow. Heidi had left a note telling Audrina to have a fabulous time. Audrina was so excited. She felt lucky to have friends like Heidi and Lauren who would help her out when she needed it.

She quickly showered and changed and then left for her date, red box in hand. Audrina and Shannon were having a low-key Valentine's Day. They had only known each other a few weeks, and Audrina didn't want to go overboard, but she still wanted to have a romantic evening. Shannon had suggested he make dinner for her at his house, and Audrina thought that was a great idea.

Audrina had never been to Shannon's house, and when she arrived, she was surprised that it was so spacious. He greeted her at the front door and ushered her inside. Shannon had made the house look beautiful with candles scattered everywhere, and he had started a fire in the fireplace. Audrina was thoroughly impressed. In front of the fireplace was a little table for two with candles on top of it. He had made a salad, garlic bread, and spaghetti. He had even made a little cake for dessert. Audrina was touched. It was all so sweet and thoughtful.

The dinner went well—Shannon was a good cook. Before he brought out the dessert, Audrina handed him the red box. He was truly surprised and touched to find a chocolate cupcake nestled inside.

"Did you make this?" he asked.

"No, my friends Heidi and Lauren did," Audrina admitted. "But it was my idea."

"It's beautiful," he said, and kissed her in thanks.

As they had done with the original cupcake that brought them together, they split it in half to eat. After she was done with her half, Audrina said, "I'm glad there was only one cupcake there that day."

"Me too," Shannon said. "Me too."

Favorite Movies

Lauren: Dirty Dancing, The Notebook

Whitney: Coming to America, My Girl, Mermaids

Audrina: Dirty Dancing, Days of Thunder, An Officer and a Gentleman

Heidi: The Notebook, all the Harry Potter movies

Fashion Emergency

Lauren and Whitney

Nicole, the *Teen Vogue* fashion editor, came into the intern closet one morning with some exciting news. Joy Bryant was going to the Oscars. Nicole explained that Joy had asked the magazine to help her find a dress to wear to all the Oscar parties she would be attending. (Joy had been the cover model for *Teen Vogue*'s December issue.)

Nicole told the girls that the fitting for the dresses would happen the following Wednesday. She asked the girls to go online and find some dresses to include in the selection they would show Joy. Nicole also told the girls that Kimball Hastings, another *Teen Vogue* editor, would be at the fitting to write a story about how Joy picked the dress and why she chose the one that she did.

After Nicole left, the girls started talking fashion. Whitney wondered if Joy would look good in a long dress or a short dress. Cocktail length or evening gown? It was an age-old question. The girls decided to find examples of both. Whitney thought Joy might look especially good in Chanel.

The following Wednesday started off as a crazy day. Earlier in the week Lauren and Whitney had done all their dress research and ran their ideas past Nicole. Then the girls contacted the designers' companies, usually dealing with the public relations department. Since everyone was looking for the right dress for the Oscars, it was competitive getting all the dresses they wanted to show Joy. But all the designers really wanted Joy to wear their creations, and the girls got every gown that they requested.

Early that Wednesday morning the girls arrived at *Teen Vogue* to prepare the dresses for Joy's fitting. Besides the new designer dresses, there were a few vintage dresses that they had found as well. The girls' job was to pack all the dresses up and then, with a couple of collapsed clothing racks and a steamer, load them all into Lauren's car and head over to the fitting. The girls soon discovered that there was no way the clothing racks were going to fit in the trunk. Lauren put the top of her convertible down and they placed the clothing racks in the backseat. The steamer went back there, too, as it needed to be transported upright so that the water in it wouldn't spill out. Thankfully, the clothes were in garment bags and fit neatly in the trunk.

The fitting was being held at Lisa Love's house. Neither Lauren nor Whitney had ever been to Lisa's house, and they got lost on the way. Twice. When they finally arrived at Lisa's home, they

were running almost half an hour late. Lauren parked the car in the driveway, and both girls unloaded the car quickly.

Lisa Love's house was stunning—it was of Spanish design and had been built in the 1920s. Whitney rang the doorbell, and Lisa let them in. Lisa didn't say anything about the lateness, for which both girls were thankful. Nicole was already there, as was Kimball, the stylist, and the photographer.

The girls put together the racks, unpacked the clothes,

and plugged in the steamer. Nicole came over to take a look at the dresses, and she liked what she saw. There was a wide selection of garments for Joy to choose from. Then Nicole asked Lauren where the red vintage dress was. Lauren looked at Whitney, who shrugged her shoulders. Nicole didn't look happy. Lauren said it was possibly in the car. She went out to look, but as she suspected, she didn't find it there. As Lauren went back into the house, Joy Bryant arrived. Lisa, Nicole, and Kimball all hugged Joy hello, and everybody talked about how great Joy looked and how long it had been since they'd seen each other.

Nicole pulled Lauren aside and asked if she'd found the red dress. Lauren shook her head no. It wasn't the end of the world according to Nicole, but it felt like it to Lauren. Luckily, Blaine hadn't arrived yet, and it was possible he could stop off at the *Teen Vogue* offices and pick it up.

Lauren grabbed her cell phone and tried Blaine's number. He didn't pick up, so Lauren left a message. As she was doing so, Blaine walked through Lisa Love's front door. It was too late. Lisa Love's house was about twenty minutes from *Teen Vogue*, so Lauren figured if she left immediately and drove like a crazy person, she could probably get the dress back to the house in time.

Lauren was about to do just that when she saw that Blaine had a garment bag draped over his arm. After Blaine said hello to Joy and the others, Lauren approached him.

"Is that the red vintage dress in there?" Lauren whispered.

"Indeed it is," Blaine replied.

"Blaine, I love you," Lauren said.

"I know."

The vintage red dress wasn't the dress Joy ended up choosing that day, although when she tried it on, she said that she loved it. Joy ultimately settled on a cocktail-length blue-and-white dress by Ralph Lauren that made her look absolutely radiant. Blaine had saved the day, and Lauren and Whitney had learned the valuable lesson of always, always checking that you have everything you need before you go to a fitting.

Lisa Love's List of Things You Shouldn't Do as an Intern

1. Don't borrow clothes from the closet.

2. Don't be late (especially to photo shoots).

3. Don't bring attention to yourself on a photo shoot.

4. Don't do anything that would embarrass the magazine.

5. Don't stop for lunch when you're on an errand for the magazine.

Thank God for Mini Golf

Lauren and Heidi

"I need some new drawers!" Heidi yelled.

"Why don't you just shout it from the rooftop," said Lauren, thankful Heidi didn't mean underwear.

"I think I'm going to go to Pottery Barn to find some drawers—wanna come?" said Heidi.

Lauren didn't have class that morning, and her shift at *Teen Vogue* wasn't until the afternoon, so she agreed to go.

Heidi was working at Privilege that night and didn't want Jordan to visit, but she didn't know how to tell him.

"The girls hit on him in the clubs, and it makes me feel like an idiot," Heidi explained.

"If you're outside all night, how do you know he's getting hit on?" Lauren asked, as she looked at a lamp.

"Elodie tells me on the walkie-talkie," said Heidi.

Heidi walked past a metal vase and accidentally bumped into it, causing it to crash loudly to the floor.

"I think you just bought that," Lauren kidded.

"Do you like it?" Heidi said dryly, as she placed the (thankfully) undamaged vase back on its stand. "Anyway, what should I do with Jordan?"

Lauren didn't have an answer, and the girls continued

furniture shopping. Heidi found a chest of drawers, a lamp, three picture frames, and some little candles.

"I can never buy just one thing here," said Heidi.

"I've noticed," said Lauren.

Just then Heidi's phone rang. It was Jordan. He had called to say that Brian had some friends in town, and Jordan was going to go out and play miniature golf with them that night. Miniature golf at night had become the thing to do in Hollywood, and Brian wanted to show his friends the newest thing. Jordan was sorry, but he wouldn't be able to stop by Privilege. Heidi pretended to be mildly upset, but told him she understood. She hung up the phone with a big smile on her face.

"What's up?" asked Lauren.

Heidi told her the good news.

"See, you were all worried, and it worked out fine," said Lauren.

"I know, and it's all because of miniature golf," said Heidi. "Who saw that coming?"

Always in My Bag

Lauren: Dior mascara

Whitney: Urban Decay blush

Audrina: M.A.C. bronzer

Heidi: Dior lip gloss

How Much for That Boggle in the Window?

Jason

"What kind of dog is that?" Jason asked, pointing to a small black-and-brown puppy.

"It's a boggle," the pet store clerk told him. "It's half Boston terrier, half beagle."

Jason had wandered into Pet Love in the Beverly Center looking for a dog. He had been thinking about getting a puggle, the popular half pug, half beagle. But when he saw the boggle, he knew that was the dog he wanted. He instantly fell in love with the cute little puppy.

The woman behind the counter said that this particular boggle was the favorite of everyone who worked at the store. She was just so cuddly and fun to play with. Jason agreed and said he'd like to buy her.

The woman said there was another buyer who had put money down on the boggle and was coming back in half an hour to finalize the deal. Jason couldn't believe it. The dog he had fallen in love with was not going to be his. He started to walk out of the pet store, dejected, when the woman ran up to him.

"There's a chance the guy might not take the boggle. He said he had to check with his son, which was why he had just put money down and didn't buy the dog outright. Why don't you check back in half an hour?" she suggested.

"Thanks, I will," said Jason, but he knew he probably wouldn't get the puppy. The boggle was so cute—what little kid wouldn't want it? Jason didn't think he had much of a chance.

He moped around the Beverly Center for another thirty minutes looking in store windows. By the time he headed back to Pet Love, he had made up his mind. If he couldn't have that boggle, he'd get another boggle instead. He'd find out if they had any more boggles coming in, and he would get the next one they had.

He walked into the pet store, ready to be disappointed. The woman at the counter remembered Jason and gave him a big smile.

"Good news—the guy's son didn't want the boggle! She's yours, if you still want her," the clerk said.

Jason took out his wallet and handed the clerk his credit card. This was turning out to be his lucky day.

A Dog By Any Other Name

Lauren and Jason

J ason loved his new dog and even liked saying "boggle" when people asked him what kind of dog it was. What Jason didn't like was that he didn't have a name for the dog yet.

Lauren's apartment complex allowed pets, and since Jason

was spending a fair amount of time there, he knew his new dog would be spending a lot of time there, too. So he decided to introduce his dog to his girlfriend. Lauren had just come in from the pool, her hair still wet, when Jason knocked on the door. Lauren opened the door and was surprised to find her boyfriend standing there holding a little dog.

"It's soooo cute! Is it a boy or a girl?" asked Lauren, taking the puppy from him.

"It's a girl," said Jason.

Lauren walked into the apartment and put the puppy down on the floor. Lauren bent down and started playing with her.

"What kind is it?" asked Lauren.

"It's a boggle, half Boston terrier and half beagle," said Jason.

Jason was in the kitchen looking for a bowl in which he could put dog food. When he found a suitable bowl, he poured the dog food into it and placed it in front of the puppy, who gobbled it up happily.

"I hope she and Bella get along," said Jason.

"What's her name?" Lauren asked.

"I have no idea," Jason said.

"She's a nameless dog?" Lauren said.

"Yeah," said Jason.

"What do you call her, when you need to call her?" Lauren asked.

"Just, Hey," Jason admitted.

"Your dog needs a name," Lauren said.

The dog continued to eat her food, spilling a bit on the floor in the process.

"She's just trouble," Jason said, as he bent down to pick up the spilled dog food.

"You should name her Trouble," Lauren said. "When you look at her, what does she look like to you?"

"I have no idea."

The dog finished eating and then started looking around the apartment. Lauren wondered if Jason was really ready for a dog.

"When it poops, it's your job and when it pees, it's your job and when it's hungry, it's your job and when it cries, it's your job," warned Lauren.

"It's cool. Me and Jordan can take 'em places," said Jason.

"You and your little dogs. It's very cute, baby," said Lauren. The dog looked up at her. "Come here, Dog Without Name." The little puppy padded over and nestled in Lauren's arms.

"Why not call her Lily?" Lauren said.

"That's perfect. C'mon here, Lily," Jason said.

And Lily jumped up into Jason's embrace.

Other Names Lauren Likes for a Dog

1. Penny
2. Trouble
3. Reese's
4. Hershey
5. Rolos

Other Names Heidi Likes for a Dog

1. Coco
2. Chanel
3. Dolce
4. Gabbana
5. Spencer

Making Copies

Whitney and Lauren

"Do you think it matters if it's not on shiny paper?" Lauren asked Whitney. The two *Teen Vogue* interns were in the mailroom, making media kits. Media kits were red binders with lots of *Teen Vogue* information inside them that were sent out to advertisers. Making them was a laborious undertaking that was sure to take a few hours even with both girls working on them. It involved a lot of copying and then cutting down the copies to fit into the binders.

"This one isn't shiny paper, so I think it's OK," said Whitney.

Lauren was at the paper cutter, while Whitney worked the photocopier.

"The blade on these things always scares me," said Lauren, as she sliced into another batch of copies.

"I know, me too," said Whitney.

"Guess what, Jason got a puppy."

"Shut up!" said Whitney.

"It's a boggle. A Boston terrier–beagle mix," said Lauren.

"I'm not really a dog person, but those are adorable," said Whitney.

"It's a cute little dog."

"I want to see it. What's its name?" asked Whitney.

"Lily," said Lauren.

"Does it poop everywhere?"

"Yeah, but it's not my dog, so I don't have to clean it up," Lauren replied.

The girls continued with their tasks. Then Lauren noticed that the paper she had been cutting down to size had a crooked edge. She was going to have to start all over again. Lauren looked at the scary paper cutter with its big sharp blade and realized the top part where she aligned the paper was crooked. Lauren made an adjustment to it, and everything was back to normal, only straighter. Whitney was impressed with Lauren's fix-it-yourself ability.

"Some of us are going to Koi tomorrow night. Would you like to come?" Lauren asked. "If you want, you can bring someone, too."

"I'm not a big sushi person, but I hear they have other food. I'd love to come."

"How can you not eat sushi?" Lauren asked.

"I've never really tried it," Whitney said.

"How can you live in L.A. and not eat sushi?" Lauren repeated.

"I don't eat sushi, and I don't eat pasta," Whitney replied, as she stood next to the copy machine.

"Those are two things I completely live off of. How can you not?" Lauren asked.

"I just don't. Sushi is so slimy, and pasta is so yeasty," Whitney said.

Lauren went back to focusing on her cutting, not believing that Whitney didn't eat sushi or pasta. Pasta! She had never met anyone who didn't eat pasta.

"I do want to go, though," said Whitney. "Koi does have other stuff, right?"

"Yeah. Do you eat any seafood?"

"Shrimp."

"They have the best shrimp. Creamy rock shrimp," Lauren said. "Maybe you'll try a bit of sushi?"

"I don't want to try any fishy ones," Whitney said.

"You can have a California roll. It's cheater sushi," Lauren said.

Whitney had grown bored of copying and now had her face pressed against the copy machine glass.

"Will you press the button?" she asked Lauren.

Lauren did as requested and out came a beautiful color copy of the side of Whitney's face.

"We should put it up in the closet," Lauren said. "A lovely picture of the weird girl who doesn't eat pasta."

Whitney rolled her eyes. "How sweet."

The Sushi Virgin

Lauren, Heidi, Whitney, and Jason

Lauren sat on the floor of her bedroom, looking in the mirror and curling her hair with a curling iron. Jason reclined on the bed on the other side of the room.

"Your hair looks just like curly fries," he said.

Lauren took a look at her curly fries hair and had to agree, but she didn't want Jason to know that. "Are you comparing my hair to fast food?" she said.

"I like curly fries," he said.

Lauren changed the subject. "You know Whitney, who I work with at *Teen Vogue*? She's going to try sushi tonight for the first time ever," she said.

"Well, Koi has great sushi, so I guess it's a good place to start," Jason said.

On the other side of the apartment Heidi was getting ready as Jordan reclined on her bed.

"I'm trying to balance everything in life right now—work, Bella, and you," Heidi said.

"I'm last, after the dog," Jordan said.

"You know I love you," she said, holding her hair high up on her head.

"You look beautiful," Jordan said. "What do you really want to do?"

"I don't know," Heidi said, as she finalized her hairdo in the mirror.

Lauren walked into Heidi's room wearing an empire-waist dress. She pulled Heidi into the bathroom and asked, "Too much boob?"

"Is there such a thing?" Heidi responded.

Soon both couples were ready to head to Koi. Jason was driving, so they all piled into his car.

Brian had already arrived and was waiting for them in front of the restaurant. Whitney was there, too, as was Audrina and a few other friends.

Inside they had a great table in one of the side rooms. It was private, but not so private that they couldn't experience the rest of the restaurant.

"This is Whitney's big night. She's going to try sushi for the first time," Lauren told everyone at the table.

Brian couldn't believe there was anyone who hadn't tried sushi. "It's the food of the gods," he said dramatically.

The restaurant was busy, as it was almost every night Lauren

and Jason had been there. Lauren liked going out with a big group of friends. It made the evening feel really special when there were more people to share it with.

Whitney was talking to Audrina at one end of the table when the sushi arrived. Whitney eyed it suspiciously. She had seen sushi before, and her brother and sisters had tried for years to bribe her into eating sushi, but now was the moment of truth. Lauren pointed out the kinds of sushi she thought Whitney might like. The California roll—or "cheater roll," as Lauren had called it—and the spicy tuna roll.

Whitney used her chopsticks to take a piece of the California roll and put it on her plate. She did the same thing with the spicy tuna roll. All eyes at the table were watching her. She picked up the piece of cheater roll and placed it in her mouth. She made a slight sour face as she chewed and then swallowed. Everyone at the table clapped loudly, congratulating her. Next came the spicy tuna roll. She put it in and for a brief moment thought about bringing her napkin to her mouth to hide her spitting it out. But she decided to stick to it and chewed and swallowed quickly, then gulped down a large glass of water. The table laughed.

"That was so bad. The rice was good, but the texture was like, yeech. I'm over it," Whitney said.

Luckily, there was the creamy rock shrimp and tons of salads and plates with cooked fish that Whitney could enjoy.

"Well, you tried it, and that's what counts," said Lauren.

Whitney agreed, feeling proud of herself for having made the effort. After all, this was L.A., where you had to try everything once.

Comfort Foods

Lauren: Macaroni and cheese, corn dogs

Whitney: In-N-Out burgers

Audrina: Chocolate

Heidi: Lobster

Maybe He Thinks You're Ugly, Too

Audrina

Audrina's younger sister, Casey, was always coming up from Orange County to visit Audrina. Casey liked hanging out with Audrina, and she loved Audrina's apartment. When she was old enough, she looked forward to getting her own place, just like her big sister.

People often thought that Audrina and Casey were twins, and Casey always took advantage of that fact. A few days after Casey's visits, Audrina would get calls from random guys saying they had met Audrina at the Beverly Center or the Grove. "Hey, Audrina, we met at the mall yesterday." But Audrina hadn't been to the mall. What had happened was that Casey would meet these guys and then give them Audrina's phone number. The really cute guys Casey would tell Audrina about, but Audrina didn't really need any help meeting cute guys.

Audrina came home from work, and the first thing she saw when she got into her apartment was a big ugly fish in a fishbowl sitting on her counter. Casey was sitting in the living room, smiling.

"I thought you might be lonely here in the apartment, so I got you a fish," Casey said.

"This is my fish?" Audrina said, stunned that her sister was giving her what amounted to a responsibility.

"I know what you're thinking," Casey said. "But it's really easy to take care of. You feed him once in the morning, and you clean the bowl out every couple of weeks."

Casey and Audrina.

OK, Audrina thought she could do that, but she didn't want a fish and she really didn't want an ugly fish.

"It's kinda ugly," she said frankly.

"That's what I thought when I first saw him, too, but then he started to grow on me," Casey said.

"Yeah, like a fungus," Audrina said.

"No, really grow. By the time I brought it here I almost kept him for myself," Casey said.

That would have been fine with Audrina. What was she going to do with a fish? Audrina walked into her bedroom to change out of her work clothes.

"I think I already have a name for it," Casey called from the living room.

Audrina walked back in from her bedroom. "You bring me a fish I don't want, and now you're going to name it, too? Somehow that doesn't seem fair."

"Elvis," Casey announced. "That's the perfect name for your fish."

Audrina liked Elvis (the singer), but she didn't want to call her ugly new fish Elvis. Audrina took a good look at the fish and said, "Samurai, that's what I'll call him."

"I don't think it's as good as Elvis, but he's your fish," Casey said with a shrug.

Just then Audrina's cell phone rang. She answered, and on the other end of the line was a guy named Frank who Audrina didn't know. Frank said they had met earlier that day at Starbucks.

Audrina handed the phone to Casey. "It's for you," she said.

Audrina had to admit she liked having her sister around, even if she did cause a bit of trouble. Audrina looked at Samurai and realized Casey was right, the fish was growing on her. He was even beginning to look cute.

I ♥ Headbands

Lauren and Heidi

"I don't know what to do with my bangs," Lauren told Heidi, as they both sat on the couch in their apartment. Lauren was looking through a pile of papers, doing skinny jeans research for *Teen Vogue*.

"Why not a Pucci scarf?" Heidi responded helpfully.

"I don't know; I did Pucci yesterday. I think I need a new headband," Lauren said.

There was a long silence from Heidi after Lauren said the word *headband*. The effect the word had on Heidi was almost mystical. Both girls loved headbands, and both girls would drop everything when the idea of going headband shopping came up in conversation.

The girls quickly got off the couch without a word, put on their shoes, and left the apartment. They were on their way to Larchmont Beauty. It was *the* beauty supply store in L.A. It had everything you could ever want, and on top of that, it was really close by.

As they drove to Larchmont, Heidi wondered out loud if Lauren had enough time to go headband shopping before she needed to be at her internship that day. Lauren said she had plenty of time, but she looked at her watch and made a frown.

"What if Marc Jacobs made headbands?" Lauren said wistfully. Marc Jacobs was Lauren's favorite designer. She simply loved everything he made.

"I saw one," Heidi said.

"Seriously?" Lauren said, snapping to attention.

"A girl at the club had it. It was red with cute little stars on it."

A Marc Jacobs headband! The very idea of it made Lauren feel like she was in heaven.

The girls pulled up to Larchmont Beauty, finding a parking spot on the street, which was never easy in the Larchmont section of town. Heidi and Lauren both liked Larchmont Boulevard. It was "neighborhood-y," which Heidi liked, and it had some cool boutiques, which Lauren liked.

Inside the beauty supply store, the girls picked up a shopping basket and made their way to the headband section.

Lauren quickly found eight headbands she needed to buy. Heidi, the conservative shopper of the two, found only four.

"What about this one for your boss, Lisa Love?" Heidi joked as she tried on a large gold headband with butterflies all over it.

"Not really her style," Lauren said. But Heidi's comment did give Lauren the idea to buy a headband for Whitney as a present. Lauren didn't know if Whitney was a headband wearer, but there was only one way to find out.

The woman behind the cash register smiled as she rang up the girls' purchases. Lauren looked at her watch and realized that she needed to hurry to get to *Teen Vogue* on time.

As Lauren got into Heidi's car she realized she had left all her skinny jeans research papers at the apartment. There wouldn't be time to go home first to get the research. Lauren didn't know what to do. If she went to work without the research, Lisa Love would think Lauren wasn't doing her job, and if she was late for work, Blaine or Lisa would call her in and ask if she was really committed to this job. Her only option was to ask Heidi for help.

"Sure," said Heidi, after Lauren explained the problem. "I'll drop you off at *Teen Vogue*, race home, pick up the research, race back to *Teen Vogue*, give you the research, and save the day."

Lauren crossed her fingers and hoped that it would all go as smoothly as Heidi had said. With Heidi, you never knew.

The first part of the plan went fine. Heidi dropped Lauren in front of the *Teen Vogue* offices. Heidi pulled the car back into traffic, barely missing a postal truck as she turned the corner.

Lauren went up to the intern closet to see that Whitney was already there. Lauren confided in Whitney that she didn't yet have the skinny jeans research that Lisa Love had asked for, but hopefully Heidi would get it to her soon.

Heidi made it back to the apartment without any other near collisions. She grabbed up all of Lauren's papers and headed back to the parking garage. As she walked to her car, a car alarm surprised her, and Heidi dropped all the papers on the floor of the garage. Heidi bent down and gathered up the papers. They looked fine, a little bit dirty from the grime on the garage floor, but fine overall.

Heidi got in her car and raced back to *Teen Vogue*. She couldn't find anywhere to park once she got to the building, so she left her car in the Blockbuster parking lot down the street. Heidi was a member of the chain video store and often rented her videos there, and because of that, figured it would be fine to park in their lot.

Upstairs at *Teen Vogue*, Heidi got off the elevator and looked for Lauren's office. She was walking through the hallway when she saw Lisa Love—and Lisa Love saw Heidi. Lisa didn't like the interns to have friends visit during the workday, and she wondered what Lauren's friend was doing in the office. She made a note to ask Lauren about it later. Lisa Love disappeared down a hall.

Heidi walked down the halls whispering, "Lauren." But Heidi

Whitney and her sister Jade shopping at Marc Jacobs.

couldn't find her. She tried calling Lauren on her cell phone, but she couldn't get a signal inside the office building.

Inside the intern closet, Whitney said that she thought she heard someone in the hallway whispering Lauren's name.

"It's probably Heidi," Lauren said.

Lauren got up from her desk and looked down the hallway. Sure enough, there was Heidi, sneaking around with Lauren's research papers under her arm. Lauren called Heidi into the intern area.

"Thank you so much," Lauren said to Heidi, taking the papers from her roommate. Then Lauren actually looked at the papers. They were dirty and out of order.

"I had a little accident in the garage at the apartment," Heidi said quickly. "The important thing is, I brought the papers here and saved the day."

"Yes, you did," Lauren said. With Heidi, you could only expect so much, after all.

"Did you like your new headband?" Heidi asked Whitney.

Whitney didn't know what Heidi was talking about. With all the skinny-jeans-research drama, Lauren had forgotten to give Whitney her surprise gift. Lauren pulled it out of her bag and gave it to Whitney.

"Thank you. It's beautiful," said Whitney, as she put it in her hair.

"And it fits," Heidi joked.

All three girls laughed. Heidi was pleased, knowing she had saved the day after all.

Guys' Night Out

Jason, Jordan, and Brian

Big Wangs in Hollywood was a sports bar with pool tables and buffalo wings, and Jason, Jordan, Brian, and their friend Kevin were there for a night out without the girls. Brian didn't have a girlfriend, and he was happy to see his friends out at night without theirs.

"Oh, Jason, I didn't recognize you without Lauren attached to you," Brian said.

"Ouch. That was kind of dick, asshole," Jason retorted.

As the four guys played pool and ate buffalo wings, they looked forward to the night ahead.

"We're going out tonight, and we're going hard," said Jordan.

"Always go hard," agreed Jason.

"Have you guys been to Lobby on Thursday night before? It is going to be raging," said Brian.

"I've been to Lobby, but I have no idea what day it was," said Jason.

Kevin was hanging back and remaining quiet. The other guys didn't mind. Kevin had agreed to be the designated driver for the evening, so the guys could have as much fun as they wanted.

"Kevin, this whole designated-driver thing is the best thing you have ever done, and I, for one, appreciate it," said Brian, meaning it.

"Hey, hey, hey, Jordan and I appreciate it, too," said Jason.

"Guys, it's my pleasure. Now, when are we gonna get the hell out of here and go over to Lobby?" Kevin said.

Right now, was the answer from the three guys, and so off they went. In the car Jordan mistakenly thought out loud, "I wonder what the girls are doing tonight." The car came to a stop.

"Tonight is about us, not your girlfriends. Got it?" asked Brian.

"Got it."

They finally arrived at Lobby, and inside the club, it was, as Brian had predicted, raging. The guys went straight inside. Kevin knew the people who worked the door, so there was never a hassle. Once inside the club, the guys headed for the VIP section upstairs.

The club was packed; even in the VIP lounge it was elbow-to-elbow. A girl approached Brian and asked him to dance. They didn't see Brian the rest of that night—he partied on the dance

floor all night long. Jordan, Jason, and Kevin finally found some free seats and sat back to take everything in.

Jason reflected that he was happy to be out with Jordan. They saw each other most days, but that was usually with the girls. Tonight was different. It was nice to be talking about sports instead of shopping.

As the three guys relaxed, just enjoying being out and having a good time, a girl came up to Jordan and asked him to dance. Jordan turned her down, but she persisted. Jordan was polite but firm. Unwilling to take no for an answer, the girl sat down on Jordan's lap. Jordan tried to gently push her off, but the girl refused to move. He stood up abruptly, which succeeded in getting the persistent girl off his lap, but as a result, she got really mad. Kevin stepped in and tried to explain to the girl that Jordan had a girlfriend, and he didn't mean to hurt her feelings. After Kevin talked to her for a while, the girl finally left Jordan alone.

"That was rough," was all Jordan said about it that night.

Downstairs, Brian had to use the bathroom. He inched his way to the men's room, and just as he got in, his Sidekick rang. Who could be calling him right now? As he entered a stall and reached for his phone, the phone fell directly into the toilet. Brian quickly fished the Sidekick out, but it would never work again. He dried it off, shoved it in his pocket, and went back out into the club. He knew that the night wasn't going to be a total loss. He was dancing with the hottest girl in the club, and the night was still very, very young. On a night like this in L.A., anything could happen.

Brian's Favorite Places to Go out in Los Angeles

1. Element

2. Privilege

3. LAX

4. Mood

5. Lobby

Burgers in Paradise

Jason, Jordan, and Brian

Astro Burger on Melrose Avenue, across the street from Paramount Studios, was *the* place to go after a night at Lobby. It was just understood: After a wild night at Lobby, you went to Astro Burger.

The sun was shining bright as Jason, Jordan, and Brian sat outside having cheeseburgers.

"Damn, this is a good cheeseburger," said Jordan, as he finished off his second one.

All three guys were wearing their sunglasses. It had been a long night, and none of them was ready for the full glare of the noonday sun.

"What was up with that girl?" Jason asked.

"What girl?" Brian asked.

"This girl tried to give me a lap dance last night," Jordan said. "It was wild."

"I think I got too drunk last night," Brian said.

"It's possible," Jason replied.

Brian had told them about the Sidekick-in-the-toilet incident; Jordan was now trying to figure out if Brian had dropped the phone in puke or urine.

"I want to say urine," Brian said.

"I need another cheeseburger," Jordan said. "You guys want anything else?"

Jason and Brian both shook their heads.

Jordan got up and went inside to the counter to get his cheeseburger. Jason wanted to know why Brian ditched them

when they got to Lobby. Brian explained that he didn't mean to ditch anybody; he just wanted to dance.

"I'm not a sit-down-at-the-table kind of guy. I like to walk around. And once I went downstairs, it was really hard to get back upstairs."

"It was a rough night," Jason said.

"I know, I haven't even been to sleep yet. I went to this after-party till about six. Then I had an audition at nine, and then I had to go to three T-Mobile stores to get a new Sidekick," Brian said.

Jordan came and sat back down with his third cheese-burger.

"Brian didn't even go to sleep last night," Jason reported.

"I slept great. Me, Bella, and Heidi all snug. Nude," Jordan said.

"Dude, I don't want to hear about a threesome involving your dog," Brian said.

"What are we doing today?" Jason asked.

"I'm going to sleep," Brian said. "I think Jordan is going to have some naked alone-time with Bella."

"Cool, I think I'll go to the movies," Jason said.

Just another day in paradise.

Jason's Best Hangover Burgers in Los Angeles

1. Astro Burger
2. Apple Pan
3. In-N-Out Burger
4. Tommy's Burgers
5. Hamburger Hamlet

Just Say No to Flip-Flops

Lauren, Heidi, and Whitney

It was another beautiful Southern California day, and Lauren awoke late. She stayed in bed to catch a few extra minutes of sleep, then suddenly remembered it was Wednesday. Wednesday! She hopped out of bed and started tearing her room apart, searching for something, anything to wear.

"What are you doing today?" Heidi yelled from across the apartment.

By this time Lauren was deep in her closet and couldn't understand what her roommate was saying.

"What?" Lauren called out while struggling with an uncooperative hanger.

Heidi opened the door to Lauren's bedroom and said in a clear voice, "I said, what are you doing today?"

Lauren, now fully awake, said, "I'm going to do that cover shoot."

"With who?"

"Ciara."

"No way! The one-two step girl?" Heidi asked.

"Can you believe it?" Lauren replied excitedly.

Lauren thought back to the previous Monday when Lisa Love and Nicole had walked into the intern closet at *Teen Vogue*, wearing very official demeanors. Lauren and Whitney looked up from their computers as the two editors entered.

Lisa spoke first. "You both remember Nicole, our features editor?"

The girls rose from their seats and politely shook hands with Nicole, who seemed pleased to be seeing the girls again.

"We have a big cover shoot on Wednesday. We're shooting Ciara," said Nicole.

"Cover shoots are very important to us," Lisa reminded the girls. "We only do ten of them a year. This is a very big deal."

In addition to it being a big deal, Lauren also knew that it was going to be a long workday, since Whitney wouldn't be there to help—she had classes all day Wednesday.

"You're going to be representing the magazine in every way at the shoot, Lauren. Please remember that," Lisa said.

Nicole promised to get Lauren more information about the

shoot by the end of the day, and then the two editors left the intern closet.

Whitney was disappointed that she wouldn't be able to assist at the shoot. "I really want to go. Maybe I should drop out of school," Whitney said.

"Bad idea," Lauren replied. One friend dropping out of school was plenty.

Back at the girls' apartment, Lauren snapped out of her reverie and redirected her attention to Heidi, who was still fixated on Lauren getting to work with Ciara.

"That is so cool. You have the best job," Heidi said enviously.

Lauren, for her part, was still trying to decide what to wear. She asked Heidi, "Do you think it's OK if I wear flip-flops?"

"Oh my gosh, are kidding me? Everyone's going to be wearing flip-flops. It's ninety degrees out. It's so hot. You'd be crazy to wear anything *but* flip-flops," replied Heidi.

Flip-flops it is, Lauren decided, picking out a pair she liked.

After a high-speed drive, Lauren arrived at the mansion in Pasadena where the Ciara photo shoot was taking place. The house was enormous—stately and imposing. Lauren gaped at it admiringly as she walked up the long driveway.

Blaine greeted Lauren at the front door of the mansion and quickly ushered her inside to meet the stylists she would be assisting that day. Heather Mary, the main stylist for the shoot, was a big deal in the stylist world, and as such she had brought two of her own assistants with her, named Jessica and Jen. Heather Mary was already down at the pool, so it was left to Jessica to show Lauren what she had to do.

Next to five racks of clothes stood a steamer. Jessica asked Lauren if she knew how to steam clothes. Lauren, all too familiar with the steaming process at this point, nodded and proceeded to get under way.

After steaming all five racks of clothes, and then another two that Jessica brought over some time later, Lauren was ready for a break. But just then Jessica walked over and asked, "Can you take these shoes down to Heather Mary by the pool?"

Lauren seized the opportunity to get away from the steamer. "Sure, only I don't know what Heather Mary looks like."

Jessica described Heather Mary as having dark hair pulled back in a ponytail and wearing a black dress. Lauren took the red Robert Clergerie heels from Jessica and headed to the pool.

Just finding the pool was an adventure. The property seemed to go on and on and on. The backyard, if you could even call it that, was the size of a public park. There were statues all over the place and manicured hedges that made Lauren feel like she was in a maze. Lauren remembered that one of the assistants had told her they used to shoot porno movies at this house. It was such a beautiful setting that Lauren had to assume a lot of "regular" movies had been shot there as well.

After some more wandering Lauren finally found the pool; now all she needed to do was find Heather Mary. There was just one problem: There were at least six women standing around the pool who fit Jessica's description of dark hair pulled back in a ponytail and a black dress. Lauren had noticed at previous photo shoots that a lot of the people on set tended to dress alike, all taking their cues from the head stylist. Surrounded by dark-haired ponytailed women in black dresses, Lauren waited with the shoes in her hands and prayed that the woman who needed the shoes would approach her instead. To her relief, a few moments later a woman came up to her and gestured to the shoes.

"The Clergeries. Thank you so much," said the woman Lauren assumed was Heather Mary.

"You're welcome," Lauren said, feeling like she was the thankful one, and handed over the red shoes.

Heather Mary turned and disappeared back into a sea of dark ponytails and black dresses.

After delivering the shoes, Lauren took the break she had been dreaming about for hours. She sat down on the low wall surrounding the Olympic-size swimming pool and rested her feet. Then out of nowhere, Lisa Love appeared.

"Lauren, what have you been doing today?" Lisa asked.

Lauren immediately got up from her seat and told Lisa, "Mostly steaming and running around. This is the first break I've had all day."

Blaine and Lauren show off their dance skills.

"I've wanted to talk to you, Lauren," said Lisa.

Lauren could feel the palms of her hands getting sweaty. She wondered what she was in trouble for this time.

"I know there are a lot of distractions for you in Los Angeles," Lisa said after a slight pause.

Lauren had no idea where this was headed. "Uh, yes," she said.

"But," Lisa continued, "I'm impressed with what you've done with your opportunities this year."

"Thank you," replied Lauren, somewhat perplexed by Lisa's statement. This wasn't the Lisa Love Lauren was used to. She was actually pleased with something Lauren had done? That was a first.

"You have a gift, Lauren, and if you keep working at it, you could go a long way in the fashion industry," Lisa said.

Now Lauren was in complete shock. She didn't know what to say, so she just stammered another thank you.

Then Lisa looked down at Lauren's feet and frowned. "Lauren, we don't wear flip-flops at *Teen Vogue*," she said disapprovingly.

Lisa turned on her expensive heels and walked away, leaving Lauren gaping behind her. Insulting her shoes! Lauren could hardly imagine anything more tragic.

Lauren's Favorite Shoes

1. Heels by Marc Jacobs

2. Flats by Steve Madden

3. Ballerina Shoes by London Sole

4. Flip-Flops by Rainbow

5. Peep Toe Heels by Steve Madden

Caught in the Act

Lauren, Heidi, and Jordan

Heidi was at work when she found out about Jordan getting a lap dance. A friend of a friend had e-mailed Heidi a link to a MySpace.com page. Heidi was bored at work that day and she had nothing better to do, so she clicked on the link. When the web page loaded, Heidi saw a picture of a girl grinding her crotch into Jordan's thigh and Jordan wearing a big smile on his face.

Heidi couldn't believe it. How could this be her Jordan? She felt hurt. She felt mad. She felt betrayed. She promptly called Jordan, but he didn't pick up his phone. He always picked up his phone, so he probably suspected that Heidi had seen the picture of the lap dance. Maybe the same friend who sent the MySpace link to Heidi had sent an e-mail to Jordan as well. Jordan probably didn't want to be put in a position where he would have to lie to Heidi about where he was and what he was doing, so it was easier to just not answer the phone.

In fact, Jordan was at the airport at that moment, picking up a girl. Heidi didn't know the girl was coming to town, and Jordan wasn't about to tell her about it until the time was right. The girl's flight landed right on time. She gave Jordan a big hug hello when she got off the plane.

"So how's Heidi?" the girl asked.

"She's great," said Jordan, just as his phone rang. It was Heidi again, but he didn't want to get it.

"Go ahead and answer it, I don't mind," said the girl.

"It's Heidi, and I don't want her to know you're here," Jordan said.

Attending a Nicole Romano fashion show.

The two of them got into Jordan's car and drove off.

Back at Bolthouse Productions, Heidi was fuming. She was telling anybody who would listen that her boyfriend, Jordan Patrick Eubanks, was in a lot of trouble. Besides the lap dance, which was awful and horrible and all of those things, now he was ignoring her phone calls! She had been trying to reach him for over two hours with no success. That was unacceptable.

Elodie, Heidi's coworker, knew that Jordan and Heidi sometimes fought, as all couples do, but Elodie had never seen Heidi this worked up in all the time they had known each other.

"I swear, he's going to be sorry he even looked at that girl," said Heidi. "Look at that smile on his face!" Heidi had printed out a couple of copies of the offending photograph so she could confront Jordan with the evidence, but right now she waved it in front of Elodie to prove her point. "There's no way he's not enjoying that."

Elodie wasn't sure what to say. "Maybe he has an explanation?" she ventured.

"He'd better," Heidi said. "Boy, he'd better. He's got lots of 'splaning to do."

Meanwhile, Jordan and the girl he'd picked up at the airport earlier had arrived at the Hillside Villas. Lauren was at the apartment, and she greeted the girl warmly.

"Holly, it's so good to see you," she said.

"It's good to see you, too, Lauren," said Holly.

Holly was Heidi's sister, and Jordan had picked her up at the airport to surprise Heidi, who had no idea that her sister was flying in from Colorado to spend a few days in Los Angeles. Jordan had planned the whole thing. Not long ago Heidi had told Jordan that she missed Holly very much and hadn't seen her in over six months, and that was way, way too long. So Jordan called up Holly the next day, and they secretly planned her visit. Jordan knew that Heidi was going to be blown away when she saw Holly, and he couldn't wait to see her reaction.

Jordan had the whole thing mapped out in his head. When Heidi arrived at the apartment after work, Holly would hide behind the door and then jump out and surprise her. It was going to be a great moment.

"I'm so excited!" Holly said as Jordan hid her suitcase in the bedroom. "I can't wait to see Heidi."

Just then Lauren's phone rang. It was Heidi. Lauren put the phone on speaker so Holly and Jordan could hear her, too.

"I am so mad at Jordan," Heidi fumed on the other end of the line. "Someone sent me a picture of him getting a lap dance. She's straddling him and he's smiling. And I've been trying to call him all day and he hasn't called me back."

Jordan put his hand to his mouth and whispered, "Oh my god."

"Oh, Heidi, I'm so sorry, what a jerk," Lauren said, glancing at Jordan.

Lauren asked where Heidi was. Heidi said she was just turning into the garage.

"I'm losing you, I'll see you in a minute," Lauren said, and hung up the phone.

Jordan looked back and forth between Lauren and Holly. "I'm not even smiling in the picture," he offered as an excuse.

"That might be the least of your problems right now," Lauren said.

Holly stared at Jordan with a how-could-you-do-that-to-my-sister look on her face. Jordan felt like all the air had been sucked out of the room. Everything seemed to be moving in slow motion. Everyone got into their places to surprise Heidi as planned, but there was no joy on anyone's face. Holly stepped behind the door while Lauren and Jordan sat down on the couch. Jordan held Bella in his lap. He told the dog, "Your mommy's gonna be very angry when she comes in in a minute."

Jordan could feel his heart beating faster. He was worried that Heidi would yell and scream, something he never really got used to from his girlfriend. Then they all heard Heidi put the key in the door. She opened the door, totally missing her sister, just as they had planned. When Heidi saw Jordan on the couch with Bella, she got very, very angry.

"Why didn't you call me back today, Jordan?" she said, through clenched teeth.

As Jordan thought of something to say, Holly sneaked up behind Heidi and tapped her on the shoulder. For a moment Heidi assumed it must be Jason standing behind her. She turned to look, and there stood her sister. Heidi gave Holly a big hug and then, because she was so excited to see her, started jumping up and down. Holly joined her. It was a funny sight, Holly and Heidi jumping up and down as they hugged. It made Jordan smile.

"What are you smiling about?" Heidi said to Jordan. "You're still in a lot of trouble." Then to her sister she said, "I cannot believe you're here. I'm so excited."

Then Heidi started crying. She hadn't seen her sister in so long, and that combined with all the crap she'd had to deal with to-

day added to the need to let the tears flow. Holly hugged her younger sister and said she didn't come all the way to Los Angeles to see Heidi cry. That just made Heidi cry more. After some more crying and more hugging, Heidi finally calmed down.

"My sister, my sister, my sister is here," she said, and then started jumping up and down again. Then, looking at her sister and speaking loudly and pointedly so Jordan would understand the meaning, Heidi said, "You can sleep in my bed."

Holly wasn't sure if this was a good idea, but she didn't say anything. Now that Heidi had calmed down from the surprise of her sister coming to town unannounced, it was time for her to focus on Jordan and the lap dance.

"I started crying at work when I saw the photograph of you and that girl," Heidi said to Jordan. Heidi took Bella from Jordan's hands and addressed the dog, "He made me cry, Bella."

"I'm sorry, Heidi," was all Jordan could say.

"It looked like you were enjoying it."

"I wasn't. She wasn't even pretty. If I'm gonna cheat on you, I'm gonna do it with a hot girl," Jordan said.

Heidi couldn't believe Jordan was being so flippant about the whole thing. "I think I'm going to throw up," she announced. She looked over at Holly for support.

Heidi's sister came over and wedged herself on the couch uncomfortably close to Jordan and then said to him clearly, "If it happens again, I'll break your nose." Then she got up from the couch and went into the bedroom to unpack.

Lauren had been quiet all this time, not wanting to get between Heidi and Jordan. She now felt like it was time to say something. They could fight about the lap dance all night and all next week—she knew how Heidi was. Lauren tried to take on the role of peacemaker.

"Heidi, Jordan planned a fun night out with Holly and everyone at Luna Park. We should probably get changed," Lauren said.

It was just the right thing to say. Heidi needed an excuse to move on. She didn't want to get into a gigantic fight with Jordan while Holly was in the next room. Heidi got off the couch, still holding Bella. She said to the dog, "Daddy totally misbehaved, but that's not going to stop us from having fun with Holly."

Lauren and Heidi went into their respective bedrooms to change for the evening, leaving Jordan on the couch, alone, to think about what he had done.

Love Means Having to Say You're Sorry

Heidi and Jordan

Luna Park was a romantic dining spot on La Brea, near Wilshire Boulevard. Jordan had read all about it and thought it would be the perfect place for Holly's welcome dinner. Audrina and Brian were meeting them at the restaurant. Jason had gone back to Laguna Beach earlier in the day and was going to catch up with them all later in the evening.

When Jordan and the three girls got out of the car in front of the restaurant, Jordan tried to pull Heidi aside to speak to her. He hadn't had a moment alone with her all day, and he wanted to apologize again, but Heidi didn't want to hear it.

"I'm trying to spend some time with my sister right now, do you mind?" Heidi snapped. Jordan gave up and held the door to the restaurant open for the three girls. They went inside to discover that Brian and Audrina had already arrived.

Usually when they all went out as a group, Heidi and Jordan sat next to each other. Lauren had once made fun of them for the habit, but they didn't stop the routine. If Heidi and Jordan were going out with everyone, they needed to sit together. Heidi was usually the one who insisted on it. Tonight, however, was different. Heidi sat down next to Lauren, with Holly on the other side. Jordan got the unsubtle message and took a seat across from her. So much for getting a moment with Heidi alone. Luna Park was loud that night, and there was going to be no way he could say anything to Heidi that the whole table wouldn't be able to hear.

Holly was introduced to Brian and Audrina, who, although they had arrived together, weren't actually "together." They had gone out on a few dates, and Brian was definitely into Audrina, but she just wanted the two of them to remain friends.

When their drinks arrived, Heidi picked up her glass and made a toast. "Here's to having the best sister in the whole wide world. Thank you for visiting me. I love you." Everyone clinked glasses and Heidi gave Holly a kiss on her check.

The waitress came over to take everyone's order. Jordan had a question about one of the items on the menu. Because it was so loud the waitress had to lean down to hear Jordan. She answered his question and then finished taking the other orders. As soon as she was gone, Heidi said to Jordan, loudly, "Did you ask her for a lap dance?"

Holly and Lauren laughed. Jordan did not.

The food soon arrived and everyone started eating. Holly loved the salad she had ordered and thanked Jordan for picking such a good restaurant. Jordan wasn't really very hungry and just picked at his food. Holly could sense that her sister wasn't going to let her anger toward Jordan fade, so she whispered in Heidi's ear, "You've got to stop being mad at Jordan."

"He always does things wrong," Heidi said.

"Guys are always going to do things wrong," Holly said.

Jordan saw Heidi and Holly whispering, and he decided it was time to make his move. He didn't care if the whole table heard him, he couldn't stand Heidi being this angry at him without him saying something. He reached across the table and took Heidi's hand and kissed it.

"I'm sorry. I really, really, really love you," he said.

Heidi got teary-eyed, visibly moved by Jordan's apology. She stood up and reached over and kissed Jordan. Everyone at the table was watching, but Heidi and Jordan didn't care. They were together, and that was all that mattered.

Fashion Forecast

Lauren and Heidi

"Hey, trend forecasting girl," Heidi said as she entered the apartment after a dip in the pool.

"How was the pool?" Lauren asked.

"You know, wet." Heidi grabbed a towel and started drying her hair.

Lauren would have loved to be out by the pool, sunning herself, but she had to finish her big trend forecasting project for school. It was an important assignment with a lot of research to be done and Lauren had been working on it for over a week.

The project consisted of Lauren figuring out something that would likely be a fashion trend a year from now. It wasn't as difficult as it sounded. Although it would help to have a crystal ball to see the future, Lauren had something else: trend forecasting books, which could predict, quite accurately, what was going to be popular in the next six months, twelve months, and eighteen months. The point of the assignment was to find a trend and then describe and expand on it, to show how it would influence a certain area of fashion.

Lauren was predicting that summer-cropped knee pants would make a big splash next spring, as would the style of clothing used in country club sports. For the project she needed to make a poster board with samples of fabrics and colors, and indicate how they each would be influenced by the trend.

The part of the project that was most nerve-wracking was that she would be expected to explain her theories to the whole class in an oral presentation.

Heidi came over to see what Lauren was doing.

"I love cropped knee pants," she said.

"Well, they're going to be huge next spring," Lauren said sourly, as she glued some fabric to the poster board.

"What kind of glue is that?" asked Heidi, as she picked up the small tube.

"It's that glue that can glue your skin together by accident. Krazy Glue. I couldn't find any other kind in the apartment," said Lauren.

"Kraziness," joked Heidi. She placed the tube of glue back down, not wanting to glue anything together accidentally.

"I guess everyone has a Krazy Glue story from when they were little kids," said Lauren.

"I don't. What's yours?" asked Heidi.

"I glued a gemstone to my head. I wanted to be like Gwen Stefani, you know, with a little colored stone on her forehead. I thought that was so cool. I found the Krazy Glue, and on the side, it said, 'Bonds to skin,' and I thought, *Well, that's what I'm looking for.* Then it wouldn't come off. My friend Jen did it, too."

"That's hilarious. How'd you get it off?" Heidi asked.

"Hot water and razor blades. That was the last time I ever glued anything to my forehead," Lauren said.

"Good thinking," said Heidi, as she headed to the bathroom to finish drying her hair.

Lauren got up early the next day to go to FIDM. She

carefully put her project in the backseat of her car. All the way to class, Lauren worried about her oral presentation. Talking in front of groups of people wasn't her absolute worst fear, but it definitely came close.

As Lauren sat in the classroom waiting for her turn, she tried to focus on her classmates' presentations. One girl talked about the influence Bollywood would have in the coming months. She had brought in a CD player and played Indian music softly in the background as she spoke. Lauren wished she had thought of something like that. But then she realized she didn't know what music she would play, because what kind of music really goes with cropped knee pants?

Lauren's name was finally called. She walked up to the front of the class with her poster board in hand. She looked out at the instructor and the other students and began her presentation. It all went perfectly. Lauren couldn't have done any better. When she finished and sat back down at her desk, it was a huge relief. All of her hard work had paid off. She found out a week later that she had received an A for her project. It was a great feeling to work so hard and then get the best grade possible. After finding out her grade, she went to the apartment complex and found Heidi lying by the pool, sunbathing. This time, Lauren joined her.

Love the Look

Lauren: Loves black, likes sunglasses by Chanel and Gucci, and of course Marc Jacobs

Whitney: Likes to wear dresses and boots when she goes out

Audrina: Her two looks are Really Pretty with a cute dress and some heels, or the whole Rock-and-Roll look with pants, boots, a cute top, and a leather jacket.

Heidi: Wears vests and boots, and thinks of herself as preppy

---

Death by Lap Dance

Heidi

With all that had been going on between Heidi and Jordan, Heidi barely had any time with Holly alone. So that Wednesday night, they decided to have a sisters-only dinner; no one else was invited.

Holly picked the restaurant: Cha Cha Cha. It was Caribbean

food, a favorite of Holly's. Caribbean wasn't Heidi's favorite, but if that was where Holly wanted to go, then so be it.

Heidi and Holly had barely taken their seats at the restaurant when Holly blurted out, "You shouldn't be so gung ho about getting engaged and married. You're nineteen. What's the rush?"

"I thought you liked Jordan," Heidi responded.

"I do. I think you guys are great together. But what if you found someone better?" Holly said.

"That doesn't sound like you like him very much. It sounds like, 'Well, he's my sister's boyfriend, so I guess I have to get along with him.' "

"That's not how it is, Heidi. I said, what *if*," Holly said.

"I've forgiven him about the lap dance. But if he gets another one, I'll kill him. It'd be like, 'Oh, what happened to Jordan?' 'Too many lap dances.' "

After the waiter took their order, Heidi tried to change the subject to Jason and Lauren. Heidi was having a hard time getting alone time with Lauren lately, because she was always with Jason.

"I wanna do a girls' night out, but there's never a good night," Heidi complained.

"Why not do it without Lauren?" suggested Holly.

"Then it wouldn't be any fun," Heidi admitted.

It seemed like the sisters weren't seeing eye-to-eye on anything. Holly wanted to know how the apartment got so messy. Heidi responded that it was clean at the moment.

"That's clean?" Holly said disbelievingly.

The girls' food arrived, and they started eating.

"I'm sorry if I came on too strong about Jordan," Holly said.

"It's OK," Heidi said.

"I just wanted you to know that just because you're not married doesn't mean you don't have a good relationship," Holly explained.

Heidi nodded. Her sister sometimes said very wise things, and Heidi understood that Holly only wanted what was best for her. It was nice having her big sister in town.

Breaking Up Is Hard to Do

Heidi and Lauren

The lap dance wasn't the only thing bothering Heidi about Jordan. He had been speaking rudely to her for the past month. Jordan's tone was getting more and more condescending, and Heidi had had enough.

She could forgive the lap dance, but how Jordan treated her on a daily basis *was* a big deal. Heidi had spoken to Jordan about it, and his behavior toward her improved, but only for a few days.

"I'm sick of it," Heidi said, as she sat down for breakfast.

Lauren was sitting across from her at the small kitchen table. "Have you tried talking to him?" Lauren asked, as she handed Heidi a bowl of oatmeal.

"Yes. He just changes for a day and then he's back to being rude."

"Doesn't sound like he's being a very good boyfriend," Lauren said.

"He's not," Heidi said, and ate a spoonful of oatmeal. "Thanks for the blueberries." Lauren had added blueberries to the oatmeal in an attempt to make it a more exciting dining experience. "I still want to go out with him," Heidi continued, "but he needs to change."

"Some boys aren't ready to change," Lauren said.

"I know, but I have to give Jordan another chance. I'll talk to him again. Maybe he'll figure out how important this is to me."

"He'd better, or it could be time for him to go," Lauren said.

"We'll see," said Heidi.

Smells Like an Ambush

Heidi and Audrina

Guy's on Beverly Boulevard was the first place Heidi hit after she and Jordan broke up. Tuesday, usually a slow club night, was when Guy's came to life with a popular karaoke night. Heidi had been wanting to go for a long time, but Jordan didn't like karaoke. Heidi could never understand that about Jordan. If he loved singing so much, why not do karaoke? Heidi was thankful she didn't have to worry about Jordan that night.

Heidi walked into Guy's ready to sing her lungs out. She loved karaoke and couldn't wait to sing. She used to go all the time back in Colorado, but could never find anyone who wanted to do it in Los Angeles. Audrina was a little less enthusiastic about going up to sing. In fact, there was no way she was going onstage. She liked going out and was happy to be there with Heidi, but she wasn't about to make a fool of herself onstage in front of a bunch of strangers.

Heidi had another reason to be excited—it was her first official night out without Jordan.

"This is going to be more fun than Taco Tuesdays," Heidi said, referring to the last time she had been out with Jordan on a Tuesday night.

Audrina nodded, even though she was actually a fan of Taco Tuesdays.

A guy who looked a little too much like Karl Lagerfeld was onstage singing "Take On Me" by a-ha.

"He sounds pretty good—maybe he can get us some Chanel suits later," Heidi joked.

Audrina didn't know what Heidi was talking about, but didn't care, as long as she didn't have to sing,

Heidi went over to the side of the stage and put her name on the list. Heidi really wanted to sing "Breakaway" by Kelly Clarkson. The two girls found a table and sat down. Audrina ordered an Arnold Palmer, and Heidi got one, too.

After the Lagerfeld guy was done, a woman got up onstage and began singing "Like a Prayer" by Madonna. Heidi couldn't believe how good the woman was. Her voice was great, and she had a whole choreography going on that didn't look like she was just making it up on the spot.

As the night wore on, Heidi and Audrina were having a lot of fun. Most of the people singing were fantastic. Then Heidi heard them call her name. No one else had sung "Breakaway" that night, so she could sing it. The club had a rule about only one version of a song a night. Heidi was fine with the rule; in fact, she was happy about it, because there are only so many times you want to hear "Stairway to Heaven" in one night.

Surprisingly unaffected by nerves, Heidi got onstage and dedicated the song to "a guy I just broke up with." Then she belted out her version of "Breakaway." Audrina was impressed at Heidi's courage, since Audrina herself would never go up there and sing.

To Audrina's surprise, after Heidi got off the stage, Audrina's name was called. It turned out Heidi had put her name on the sign-up sheet without telling her. Audrina didn't raise her hand or walk onstage. Heidi pointed to her and told the crowd, "That's Audrina. She's a little shy, so how about some help?" Everyone else in the club started clapping their hands and chanting Audrina's name.

Slowly, Audrina stood up and walked to the stage. As she passed Heidi she said under her breath, "You're dead."

Once onstage, Audrina learned she'd be singing "Smells Like

Teen Spirit" by Nirvana. She started off slowly, but by the time the chorus came around, everyone in the club was cheering her on. By the time the song ended, Audrina had sweat pouring off her. She walked off the stage to thunderous applause. Back at the table Heidi asked if she had fun. Audrina admitted that she did and took a sip of her drink.

"I need something stronger than an Arnold Palmer after that," Audrina said.

Heidi called the waitress over for her friend.

Boba, Boba, Boba

Lauren and Whitney

On her way to the *Teen Vogue* offices in the morning, Whitney would often stop at a place called Zen Zoo and get a drink called the Dragon. It was made with mint tea and at the bottom of the drink were little black pearls of tapioca called Boba.

Whitney soon became addicted to the Dragon and started having one every day. She would find reasons to drive by Zen Zoo and then stop in for the Dragon. Some days she would have a salad or edamame as well, but let's face it, she was really there for the Dragon.

One day she mentioned the drink to Lauren.

"What's that?" Lauren asked.

"You don't know Boba? Shut up! You have to come with me to get some," said Whitney, excited by the prospect of introducing Lauren to her new addiction.

Whitney was eager for the Bobafest to begin, so she planned on meeting Lauren at Zen Zoo the next day before work.

The girls pulled into the Zen Zoo parking lot at exactly the same time the next morning. After checking with Lauren to see if she liked mint, which she did, Whitney ordered for both of them. The Dragons came in clear plastic cups.

"That's the Boba," said Whitney, pointing to the little black balls in the bottom of the cup. Lauren looked at the drink skeptically. She didn't mind trying new things, but this drink looked downright weird. Whitney handed Lauren a wide straw to put into the top of the cup. Whitney then explained that you had to drink it through a straw to get to the Boba. Lauren noticed that Whitney was getting excited. Each time Whitney said Boba, her voice quivered and changed octaves.

Lauren put the straw in the drink and gave it a try. The mint tea was delicious, and then up through the straw came one of the black things, the Boba, into Lauren's mouth. It had an odd rubbery texture.

"I'm supposed to chew this?" Lauren said, with the Boba in her mouth.

"Yes," said Whitney. "It's super delicious."

Lauren chewed tentatively, and the sweetness of the Boba quickly became apparent.

"This is pretty good," Lauren admitted.

Whitney was pleased. "We'd better get going; we don't want to be late for work."

As they headed to the parking lot, Lauren was thankful that Whitney was her friend. Sure, Whitney could be kind of kooky sometimes, but Lauren really liked that about her. You just never knew what to expect where Whitney was concerned.

"Thanks for the Boba introduction," Lauren said, before she got into her car.

"My pleasure. See you at the office," Whitney said.

Both girls got into their cars and drove off toward the *Teen Vogue* building with their Boba drinks beside them. Lauren was psyched to have discovered yet another thing she loved about L.A.

Call of the Road

Audrina

Shannon's band, 30 Seconds to Mars, was rehearsing at one of the larger rehearsal spaces in Hollywood. The city had hundreds of little soundproof rooms that were rented out by the hour or the day. Inside these rooms, on most days, you could find bands practicing. Good bands, bad bands, bands that were struggling, bands that had made it, even bands that had made it and were now struggling. Shannon's band was a good band—Audrina thought so, at least, and evidently she wasn't alone, as the band was having amazing success lately—so much so that the band had decided to go out on tour. They needed plenty of rehearsal time first, however, which was why the boys of 30 Seconds to Mars were currently playing their songs in the middle of the day in a rehearsal room in Hollywood.

Audrina sat on one of the three couches in the room with a

few friends of the band and listened to them rehearse. Shannon sat behind his drum kit, unleashing a fury on the drums. Sweat was pouring off of him. Being in a band was hard work, Audrina mused. Being the drummer seemed extra hard, since the drummer had to keep the beat steady and clear throughout every song so the rest of the band could follow along. The last time Audrina stopped by to listen to rehearsal, Shannon had shown Audrina all the different drums he had and how he used them. It seemed like a complicated process.

Shannon and the band were leaving the next day on their tour, and because Shannon was so busy with preparations, this was where Shannon and Audrina were going to have to say good-bye. The band came to the end of the song, and they called a ten-minute break. Shannon stepped out from behind the drums and hugged Audrina. His shirt was completely soaked through with sweat, but Audrina didn't mind. They walked out to a lounge area next to the rehearsal room.

The lounge had a soda/water machine, and Shannon put in some money and pressed a button for a water.

"Do you want anything?" he asked Audrina.

"I wish these machines had Arnold Palmers in them," she said.

"That would be great. You know Roscoe's House of Chicken N Waffles?" Shannon said.

"I've heard of it," Audrina responded, not sure where this was going.

"They serve lemonade and iced tea there, but they don't call it an Arnold Palmer," Shannon said.

Audrina was incredulous. "What do they call it there?" she asked.

"Lisa's Delight. I had one the other day and thought of you."

Audrina was touched. She was going to miss Shannon while he was on tour.

"What are you gonna do while I'm gone? I mean, besides miss me," Shannon joked.

"I don't know," Audrina said, suddenly feeling tears welling up.

Shannon put his arms around her comfortingly. He held her like that until someone from the rehearsal room called out to Shannon that they were starting up practice again.

Audrina kissed Shannon tenderly and said good-bye. She knew they would see each other again. She just didn't know when, and that was the hard part. She wasn't looking forward to diving back into the dating pool, but if she had to, she would. She certainly knew her way around the pool by now.

No Ex-Boyfriends Allowed

Heidi and Jordan

Wednesday night was LAX night, and, as usual, Heidi was working the door. She hadn't been single very long, but her whole attitude about working the clubs had changed. Even her coworker Elodie had noticed it. Heidi was even more flirtatious than usual, in an attentive and lighthearted way that charmed the guests.

"You seem like you're having more fun out here," said Elodie that night.

"I am. I'm talking to more guys and not feeling guilty about it," said Heidi.

"That's a good thing," Elodie said, and went back into the club.

As Heidi was checking people's names on her clipboard, she saw Brian walk past out of the corner of her eye. She called out his name, and he stopped and looked around for the source of the voice. When he saw Heidi, he walked over to her and gave her a hug.

Heidi hadn't seen Brian since she and Jordan had broken up; she hoped it wouldn't be awkward. But she needn't have worried—Brian was a perfect gentleman.

"It's good to see you, Heidi," Brian said.

"You too," Heidi said. "Are you coming into the club tonight?"

"I'm thinking about it. You think you could get me in?" he said.

Heidi told him that she could, if he was interested. They

Jordan takes a break between rounds of golf.

talked a bit more, mostly about Brian and his movie and how he was thinking of doing more stand-up. Neither of them mentioned Jordan. Finally, they said good-bye, and Heidi told the doorman to let Brian into the club.

A few minutes later Jordan walked up and said hello. Heidi was surprised to see her old boyfriend there, but wasn't really unhappy about it. They shared a brief awkward hug.

"So what brings you by tonight?" Heidi asked. "Your room-mate's already inside."

"Yeah, I know," said Jordan. He was quiet for a moment, trying to think of something to say. "I just want you to know I'm sorry, Heidi," he said finally.

Suddenly Heidi felt like maybe it was a little too soon to be seeing her ex after all. She didn't want to be rude to him, but she also didn't want to rehash their breakup at the front door of LAX.

"Jordan, look, it's good seeing you and everything, but I have to work. Do you want to go into the club?" Heidi said briskly.

Jordan was taken aback by Heidi's businesslike manner, but if that was how she wanted to play it, that was fine with him. He told Heidi he did want to go into the club, and once he was inside, he wandered around until he found Brian standing at the bar.

"How'd it go with Heidi?" Brian asked, shouting over the loud music.

"OK," said Jordan. "I think she has a lot of growing up to do."

Brian nodded, and Jordan ordered a drink.

Outside, Heidi continued working, consulting her clipboard and letting other guests into the club. But her encounter with Jordan still bothered her. She knew there was an unofficial rule the girls of Bolthouse had when working clubs: No Boyfriends Allowed. But now she wanted to make a new rule: No Ex-Boyfriends Allowed.

Never Turn Down
a Free Haircut

Audrina

Audrina was working extra hours at Quixote Studios. They had asked her to come in on a weekend to help out, and Audrina didn't mind. She liked the people at the studio, and if they needed some extra help, she was happy to assist.

That Saturday a sneaker commercial was being filmed on stage three. Audrina knew some of the people working on the commercial, so at least she'd have someone to talk to during the day.

As Audrina sat at the receptionist desk, a handsome dark-haired guy walked up to her and asked if she had any more magazines. His name was Justin, and Audrina thought he was kind of cute. *But magazines?* she thought. *He couldn't come up with a better pick-up line than that?* It had to be his version of a pick-up line, judging from the way he was staring at her and the fact that he had just passed by two tables with magazines spread all over them. Audrina played along and pointed out the tables with the magazines, but Justin lingered. He told her he was the hairstylist on the shoot (although not the same hairstylist named Justin who had cut Lauren's hair for *Teen Vogue*), and then offered to cut her hair, if he had any extra time that day. Audrina thanked him and then went back to work.

Justin stopped by three more times during the day. "I'm really busy right now, but there may be time to squeeze you in at the end of the day," he said.

Audrina smiled noncommittally each time. At the end of the day, he said he had an appointment waiting, but if he could get her number he would call and set a time to do her hair. He seemed like a nice enough guy, so she handed him her number on the back of a business card.

Justin called two days later, and they set up a time for him to do her hair. Audrina wasn't sure about inviting him over to her house, but she didn't want to do it at work, and she needed to get home to look after her new kitten. Two weeks earlier a friend's cat had given birth to kittens, and the friend had asked Audrina if she wanted one. Audrina loved cats, and so had said yes right away. She decided that although it wasn't ideal, it was easiest to just have Justin come to her apartment.

Audrina's apartment in the complex can be difficult to find, and Justin had to call after he parked to get directions to Audrina's door.

Audrina was holding the kitten when she let him into her apartment. They discussed what to do with her hair, and then Justin asked if he could hold the kitten. Audrina handed her over to him.

As he was playing with the kitten, he said, "It's got a little kink in its tail, feel."

Audrina did as she was told, and sure enough, there was a little ridge near the end of the kitten's tail.

"Do you have a name for her yet?" Justin asked.

Audrina admitted that she didn't—she just hadn't thought of a good one yet.

"You should call her Kinky," Justin suggested.

"My dad wants me to call her Twiggy," Audrina said.

"No, you should call her Kinky," Justin said.

Kinky is not an acceptable name, thought Audrina. "I think I'm going to go with something else," she said diplomatically.

The conversation moved back to Audrina's hair. Justin

thought a slight trim to add some volume would be good. Audrina agreed, and Justin got to work. The haircut turned out to be one of the best Audrina had ever received; she wasn't sure if she would see Justin again for a date, but she was definitely happy about the haircut. Justin hugged her good night and left the apartment. Audrina decided to take a wait-and-see approach with him. If he called again, she might be open to it, but if he didn't, that was OK, too.

She ended up calling her kitten Betsey, after her favorite designer, Betsey Johnson, which was a *much* better name than Kinky, in Audrina's opinion. This Justin character didn't seem to know much about cats—or women for that matter—but at least he'd given her a great haircut.

Bet You Didn't Know

Lauren: Likes to call Jason Bub or Bubby as a pet name

Whitney: Used to go to every 'NSYNC concert

Audrina: Thinks of herself as very competitive

Heidi: Was so nervous during her Bolthouse job interview she thought she was going to wet her pants.

Declaration of Independence

Heidi and Audrina

Heidi and Audrina were having a fun night. Earlier in the evening they had gone out to dinner at Mandarette, and while they were ordering, the guys at the next table started hitting on them. Heidi enjoyed flirting, and now that she wasn't with Jordan anymore, she could do it guilt free. The guys turned out to be lame, but it was still fun while it lasted.

When they got back to the Hillside Villas, the two girls

decided to go in the hot tub. They hadn't been in the hot tub in forever. Not for a month, at least, and that felt like forever to Heidi. The two bikini-clad girls eased themselves into the hot tub as they engaged in girl talk.

The topic of discussion was whether either girl had a "type." Audrina didn't think she had one, although she did find herself gravitating toward guys in bands or guys that look like they're in bands.

Heidi didn't think she had a type, either. "I mean, I've dated Italian boys, I've dated skater boys, and I've dated all-American football boys. You know, I've dated every kind of boy you can think of, but in the end, what's important is how a boy treats you," Heidi said.

Audrina nodded. "I always seem to go for the bad boys. I get bored easily, so if they don't keep me on my toes, I'm out of there."

That's a good method to figure out when you want to leave a relationship, thought Heidi: *Boredom.*

Heidi began telling Audrina about the worst date she had ever had. It had been while she was living in San Francisco.

"I was so bored, I thought I'd crap myself," said Heidi.

Audrina laughed loudly.

"He went up to go to the bathroom, and I called my friend and told her to call me in five minutes and pretend there was an emergency," Heidi said. "So she called me, and then I told the guy, 'I'm so sorry, I have to go, bye.'"

"That sounds like a good one," said Audrina.

"All he did was talk about himself. Remembering it now makes me have throw-up in my mouth," said Heidi.

Audrina giggled. "I hate guys that just talk about themselves," she said. "It's just arrogance, and then when you talk they don't listen."

"I think that's called being a guy," Heidi joked.

Audrina thought back to all the bad dates she had experienced with lame actor types—guys who were so into themselves that they don't really have time for anything else.

"Isn't being single great?" said Heidi sarcastically.

"Are you saying you'd rather be back with Jordan?" Audrina countered.

"God, no. This past month has been the best month of my life. No one to answer to. No one yelling at me. Things are good. In fact, I met a guy I kind of like," said Heidi.

"Who is it?"

"A guy I met at Privilege. His name is Spencer."

"I knew it! I knew you seemed extra happy the past couple of days," said Audrina.

"Yeah, I like him, but you know, I'm not looking to settle down," said Heidi.

"Who is?" said Audrina, and both girls laughed. It looked like it was going to be a fun summer after all.

Heidi's Six Favorite Things About Being Single

1. No one to answer to

2. You can do anything you want.

3. There are millions of hot guys.

4. Free dinners

5. You can have so much fun with your friends.

6. You have more time for yourself.

The Rest Is Still Unwritten

Lauren, Heidi, Audrina and Whitney

They had been in Los Angeles for less than a year, but all four girls had grown so much. Heidi once thought she couldn't live without her boyfriend, but now she was thrilled to be a single girl for the summer. Whitney was back in Los Angeles where she belonged, and her junior high school crush was now her college boyfriend. Audrina had learned that not every guy deserved to be trusted; she was smarter now and not so gullible.

Of all the girls, Lauren had come the farthest. Summer was just beginning, and she finally had the three things for which she came to Los Angeles: a great education, a killer job, and a boyfriend who made her happier than anything else in the world. She knew she'd better enjoy it while it lasted: Things happen lightning-fast in Los Angeles, and in a flash her academic life, her job—even her relationship—could fall to pieces.

This felt like the end of a chapter for all of them, but it was not the end of their stories. These girls had many adventures left to live, and this was the City of Angels, where anything could happen. The next chapter was just beginning.

Acknowledgments

Many thanks to Brent Bolthouse, Lollion Chong, Lauren Conrad, Tony DiSanto, Adam DiVello, Brian Drolet, Jordan Eubanks, Liz Gateley, Jennifer Heddle, Jacob Hoye, Bill Langworthy, Lisa Love, Heidi Montag, Elodie Otto, Audrina Patridge, Whitney Port, Sophia Rossi, Dave Sirulnick, Sean Travis, Jason Wahler, and Blaine Zuckerman.